Enter My Life

Aisia Bell

Copyright © 2024 Aisia Bell

All Rights Reserved

ISBN:

Dedication

I want to dedicate the book to my kids, God, the bells, my mom and my siblings.

Acknowledgment

I want to acknowledge my teachers in school, the counselors who helped me at the Kare house, my church, Megan Morrow and Monica.

CONTENTS

Dedication iii

Acknowledgment iv

About the Author vii

Chapter 1 - The Beginning 1

Chapter 2 - All Grown Up Now 8

Chapter 3 - Giving Up 18

Chapter 4 - I'm Too Broken 23

Chapter 5 - See You Again Someday Auntie 29

Chapter 6 - The K.A.R.E House 33

Chapter 7 - Becoming An Adult 41

Chapter 8 - Senior Year 45

Chapter 9 - Leaving My Mom's House 48

Chapter 10 - Meeting My Future Family 54

Chapter 11 - Meeting My Kids' Father 60

Chapter 12 - Being A Mother 69

Chapter 13 - What Do I Do Now 75

Chapter 14 - My Own Place 85

Chapter 15 - Margarita, I Do Love You 89

Chapter 16 – My Little Surprise 95

Chapter 17 – A Whirlwind 99

Chapter 18 – How Did I Get Here 105

Chapter 19 – Being Who I Was Meant to Be 109

Chapter 20 – I Have To Leave 115

Chapter 21 – A New Life 120

Chapter 22 – My Own Place Again 124

Chapter 23 – He Saw Me 129

Chapter 24 – What Are the Odds 131

Chapter 25 – What Kind of Big Sister Am I 140

About the Author

I am a 38-year-old single mother who loves to help people who go to church every Sunday. I just love to write and help the next person who's going through something. My life is mostly just being a single mother.

Chapter 1 - The Beginning

Hi, my name is Aisia Emma Bell (a.k.a) Iesha. I was born on a Tuesday at 11:30 am March 4, 1986. I was born to an 18-year-old woman. Her name was Rachel Mary Bell. It was just my mommy and me for a while. We lived with my grandmother Laura at her house. We lived there until my mother got her place. My father left us. I did not even know his name. All I knew was he was a Puerto Rican guy. My mommy said I used to stay with his mother, but I do not remember her either. At a later point, my father came back to us. My mommy got pregnant with twin boys. But my father left before the twins were born. When I was one year old, my mommy got her apartment. My mommy and I moved to 265 Broadway, Bayonne, New Jersey. At the age of one, I started to have seizures. Also, that same year, my mommy and my father had twin boys. Their names were Terry and Jerry Bell. Immediately after they were born, they were given to an adoption agency, so I do not know if their names have been changed. So, if you are keeping track, my father was gone, and my two brothers were gone. My father's leaving made me believe there was something wrong with me. I thought that if he left, that meant he did not want me.

When I turned three, I went to a child daycare center. At that daycare center, they gave me a test on my walking ability, and they put braces on my legs. Because at three years old, I was still crawling and scooting on my backside, I did not walk. In addition, I did not talk. I did not even play with the other babies. I thought, there goes my future, an introvert in the making. They also gave me a test on my intelligence. They said I was borderline intelligent. And after a few months, they took the braces off my legs.

When I turned four years old, Anthony Jerome Fields came into our lives. I remember there was a knock on the door. I thought I was a big girl, so I ran to the door and opened it. This tall black man was standing in front of me. From behind me, my mommy said, "Oh, come on in, Anthony." It was no longer Mommy and me because there was now a man in our house. That was it. He came into a ready-made family. At first, Anthony was a great stepdad. I even remember one time when we were walking to my grandmother Laura's house, and Anthony put me up on his shoulders. I do not know if I was walking slowly or if I was tired, but he did it. He put me up on his shoulders. Like I said, he was a great stepdad until he had his kid.

When I was five, Anthony and my mommy had Anthony's first daughter, Essie Antoinette Bell (a.k.a. Es). When she came home from the hospital, I was the first one that got to hold her. When I looked down at her beautiful face, I knew I was to protect her at all costs. She was my gift. Essie was allergic to all the infant milk at that time, and she was very sick. One night, my mommy was having a hard time trying to put her to sleep. And I guess I was making too much noise so mommy asked Anthony to take me to the store. At this time, Anthony had a car, and he let me sit in the front seat. I felt like a big girl.

When I was six years old, mommy and Anthony had Anthony's second child, Mary Antonio Bell (a.k.a. Mar-to-more). A year later, they had Anthony's first son, Anthony Jerome Bell (a.k.a. Ant). One year after that, Mommy and Anthony had their last child together,

Patrick Jerry Bell (a.k.a. Patty Pat). Each time my mommy went into the hospital to have one of my siblings, I went to either the upstairs neighbor's house or my Grandma Laura's house. When I heard I had another sibling, I would run home to see them. I was always the first one to hold them. My little siblings were my first kids.

As they became family with my mommy and their father, I became the outsider, the loner, the weird one. Each of my siblings had a distinct personality. Essie was the princess who could do no wrong. Mary was the spoiled brat and got everything she wanted. Anthony was a manly man; no matter what, he would not cry for anything. And Patrick was the baby and we all protected him. You probably want to know about the twins. As I mentioned, Mommy put them up for adoption, and we never got to know them. As for me, well, I told you that I am the outsider, but being their big sister meant everything to me.

Since I told you about my siblings, let me tell you about the rest of the Bells. I never got to meet my mommy's dad, whose name was Raymond. He died when my mommy was pregnant with me. But my mommy's mom was grandmother Laura were the best. She was my everything. Grandma Laura was the one person, and her house was the one place I felt safe. I felt I could be myself.

I could go to her house and run to her bed no matter if she was sleeping; she would say, "Come on, my little white baby, get up here," Grandma Laura had a way of making me just go to the park and adventure.

My uncles and aunts on my mother's side were the best. They are the reason I am so family-oriented now. I am sure I got my swagger from my uncles because no one is cooler than them. Generation one, you really are the best!!! My family is big. Let me tell you how big we are. My grandma and grandpa had 12 kids. We call them Generation One. Combined, Generation One had about 50 to 60 children, and Generation Two. I am a partof generation two. Combined, we had about 100 to 200 kids; they were Generation 3. Some of Generation 3 had about ten kids. So yeah, we are a big family. The cousins that I grew up with were wonderful. They are loud and opinionated, and they do not back down. I guess that was because of our parents. But we are also caring, loving, and kind. I guess that is because of our parents also. Isn't it funny how you could be from such a big family and feel so alone? Ok, maybe not ha ha funny, but interesting.

I remember one birthday, my cousin Candie and I had our party together. Candies and I birthdays are two days and a year apart. Candie'sbirthday was March 6, 1987. Mine is March 4, 1986. Everyone was their cousins, aunts, uncles, and my grandma Laura. I remember my cousins Velda and L. A took us younger cousins to the park across the street. It was Velda, LA, Veda, Christina, Candie and me. We played until it got dark. Then Velda yelled we better get back before we get in trouble. So, we all ran to Grandma Laura's house. When we got there, it was even more crowded with family and close family friends. They put on my song "Iesha" by another bad creation. That is my family name. If you call me that you must be either family or knew the family so long you are a Bell by extension. That's why I said hi; I'm Aisia Bell {Iesha] because I am. It's a blessing and some would say a curse to have a family name because that's who I am, and I always will be their little Iesha. Let me get back to the party. We ate, laughed, joked, and were merry. That's the thing: you don't have to give the Bells a reason to celebrate. We can celebrate even if the only reason is because it's Tuesday.

After that party, my lovely grandma Laura started to get sick. Grandma'shouse was where we all went. I remember when I was three, I was at grandma's house, and I decided that I was going ride my big wheel in her hallway. It was all fun until my mom came back from work to pick me up. As you may believe, she was not happy. She grabbed me and my big wheel. She took us inside the house and asked who let Iesha ride her big wheel in the hallway. I got away from Mommy and ran to Grandma. And she said, come here, my little white baby. She told my mom to leave me alone and that I was just playing. I remember one day, my uncle stole boxes from ShopRite. That's all he got: a bunch of boxes. Nothing was in there when he was asked what happened. And how he just took boxes. He said because he had to run. And I guess he was able to because he only had empty boxes. So yeah, Grandma's was headquarters. So, when Grandma passed away, we didn't have a headquarters anymore. My grandmother had a boyfriend while she was alive. I thought he was mean. I remember one day, I was at grandma's house. MY cousins and I were sitting on the sofa. It was Christina, Candie and me. Grandma's boyfriend just mops the floor. We played I Triple Dog Dare You to see who was going to walk on the floor. But we all knew none of us was going to.

Even though she got sick, she still did things with our grandkids, but it was not as much. I remember one day, Grandma took us grandkids to the park across the street from her house. I remember looking up at her and thinking she could touch the sky. I thought she was so tall nothing couldtouch her that she would be there forever. But that's not how the world works. That random morning was one of her last. I don't remember who else came with us. All I remember is that I got to hold my grandmas. Then, Grandma was on bed rest. Then she went to the hospital. Then she was gone.

One day, my mom said my lovely grandmother Laura passed away. My dumb self-thought, she said, passed out. Remember that because then you understand this paragraph. So, we got up and got dressed to go to the church. At the front of the church, there was this wooden box. In that box was my grandmother. Everyone went up to see her. My mom is in front of me then it's my turn.

All I was thinking was, "Grandma, I don't like this place. Get up so we can go home," but she did not get up.

So, then we had to sit down. My cousin Velda sang"Angle of Mine" by Monica. Then we went to the burial site. The Preacher preached. We said goodbye, and those mean men threw dirt on the box that my grandma was in, and we left. We just left her there. We went back to her house, but I did not feel safe. Something was different. I did not think I would feel safe again. Again, everyone was everywhere, but it was not the same. I asked my mom when we were going to get grandma; she said we were not. I remember looking out the window where the fire escape was. Just looking outside think like she is supposed to be here. It was her apartment. I remember everyone drinking, laughing, and being Merry, but I did not think we were supposed to. I thought we just left your mother, grandmother, cousin, aunt, sister. What is wrong with you? I do not remember leaving Grandma's house, but I know we did. That was the last day of my "childhood."

Chapter 2 - All Grown Up Now

Grandma died when I was seven. She never got to meet Patrick. Anthony was a baby. Essie and Mary were so young that they do not remember her, but I do. When I was eight, I knew I was different than the other girls. It was not just I did not like makeup. It was not that I did not like dresses. It was not because I was a "tomboy." I knew what it was, and I hated myself for it. I had this biggest crush on my best friend from school, named Rosanna. I didn't know what it was, but I knew I wanted to kiss her like mommies and daddies do. I was so drawn to her. She was the bad girl. She was the one who said what was on her mind; even if it was to bring me down, I did not care. At least she was talking to me. Can you say toxic?

But I wanted her to be my girlfriend. The problem was she was she, and so was I. I did not tell anyone. I couldn't even say it to myself, let alone my mom. My mom was not the person to talk to about this. No one knew. For a while, I didn't want to know. I remember when I used to spend a night a Rosanna's house. There was one Sunday I was supposed to be home. I just walked around the block a couple of times, praying that it would be Friday again, just not to go home because it wasn't a good place to be in. My mom came in a cab to find me, and she found me then. She said that she called Rosanna's mom to see where I was. Rosanna's mom said that I had left a long time ago. So, she came to find me.

There was this other Sunday I was supposed to go home, but Rosanna's mom called my mom and asked if I could stay another night because we wanted to stay at this ladies' house. My mom said yes, so Rosanna and I went to the lady's apartment upstairs in Rosanna's building. She let us in, and we ate dinner. She said she was like an aunt to Rosanna. I felt comfortable enough to tell her what was going on at my house. I told her when I would wet the bed, I would get beat or my glass dolls broken on my legs by my stepdad. That hurt, but what hurt the most was when he would make my mom do it. Because until she did, I could pretend she was on my side. The thing was, I would wet the bed because I was scared.

The lady said she would adopt me, and I never had to go back there. I was so happy, like I was happy to live with this stranger like I met this lady not even two minutes ago, but I was ecstatic. She gave me a watch to show me that she was going to fight for me. We went to bed. I woke up in the morning and went to school thinking, soon, I will be out of there.

Rosanna came to school and said, "I told her you lied," and "she wants her watch back."

I cried and returned it. I understood as I was going that I would not survive. I knew that I would die. But since Rosanna was ignorant, I was unable to hold her accountable. When she saw the lovely, caring, and kind mother, she assumed it was the mother I always had. She didn't ever see my dad. She was thus ignorant. We remained friends.

When I was nine, everything changed for me. One day, my friend Susan asked me to spend a night at her father's house with her. I thought this was weird as her best friend was Nicole. But I went anyway. In hindsight, I shouldn't have gone.

Well, I ran upstairs and asked my mom, "Can I go?"

She said, "Yes."

I ran, got my clothes, and went back downstairs. Once I was in the car, I didn't get out. Upon returning, they found a different person. In other words, the daughter who returned was not the same child who departed.

She was stuck in that car. Susan's dad, "George," Susan and I went to shop rite. We got a lot of junk food and headed to his house. We got there, ate the food, played, and had a great deal of fun. Then it was bedtime, so Susan and I went to bed, too. Again, I should have known it was weird that there was one bed, one bedroom. But I thought that Susan didn't live with him 100%, so maybe that's why. We went to bed, and I fell asleep fast.

In the middle of the night, I woke up to my hand rubbing Susan's backside. I sensed something more than George's hand was resting on mine. He must have sensed my nervousness because he pulled me towards him and his daughter.

"I should touch him," he said. "I should suck him," he said.

That evening, I followed instructions. I don't recall returning to sleep. Though I doubt I did. But nobody mentioned anything when I got home the following day. We simply ride in quietly to 11th Street.

I went into my building, walked upstairs, and entered into my apartment. I got into the shower and cried silently. Then I got out of the shower, but the child that I was was dead.

My mom asked, "How was your night?"

I said, "It was fine."

She asked, "Did you have fun?"

I said, "Yeah, it was fine."

I know you are probably wondering why I didn't say anything. Well, my mom was not the person you talked to about that. I didn't feel safe with her. I knew she wouldn't do anything. No matter what she said then. My grandma was that person, and she was gone.

So, I said it was fine, "OK, let's talk about my mother."

All you readers need to understand her more to understand the rest of my story.

I was born to my mother when I was eighteen. At seventeen, she became pregnant with me. She used to say to me that she was glad she had a daughter since she had desired one. I don't believe I'm the daughter my mother desired. I used to be her best friend, she used to claim. That's what I had, then. I was born to a friend of mine. Mary, Patrick, Anthony, and Essie all had a mother. My mother would come to me with her anxieties, fears, and concerns. Not every moment my mother was in our world.

I had to find things for her a lot. The blame had to fall on me. Because she's my mother, I did it. She once sent me across the street to check on my aunt's spouse, as I recall. I would do it even though I knew everyone was staring at me because we needed food. Ignore them, though, as nobody assisted the 7, 8, 9, 10, 11, and 12-year-old. They did nothing but watch me wait outside in the bitter cold until I decided it was long enough to go back inside. I can thus affirm that he was present and that he would feed us.

One time, I was done with being in that house, so I told her that he wanted me to go to my aunt's house. So, she let me go. So, I went. I was about 10. I knew how to get there. I didn't know what to tell my aunt, but I needed to go. So, I got there. I went to her apartment and knocked on the door. No one was home. So, I went outside, sad that I had to go back home. When I saw my aunt, I was so happy.

She said, "Iesha, what are you doing here?" and "Where is your mom?"

I told her why I was there and that my mom was home.

She shook her head and said, "OK, come on in."

To this day, that was the best thing she could have done.

"Thank you, Aunt Lizzy."

I remember after D.Y.F.S came into the picture, there was some kind of smell in the house.

The homemaker said, "It smelled like a man."

And, of course, they came to me and asked me who I let in the house.

I said, "No one; I was asleep."

But to get someone to say anything you want them to be keep asking the same question. That is what they did.

"So, I finally said, "Yes, it was me."

So, they asked, "Who?"

And my mom asked, "Was it your dad?"

Then she knew I didn't know that Puerto Rican guy. It didn't matter because she changed that quickly. After all, all I did was look at her like, really. Then she said something in front of the caseworker that she should have never asked. She asked if I let the D.Y.F.S worker sept son in the house. To understand why she asked that question, it was because they were unprofessional, and we went to their house and knew their family.

I thought like why? How am I supposed to get you out of this one? But I think she was trying to get me out of the endless questions. Because the caseworker laughed like she truly contacted the D.Y.F.S. worker and stopped asking me questions, I had to listen to that and laugh all day long. They were making fun of my mother. That's when I started to fight since nobody was going to make fun of me in that way. Yes, there were issues in my connection with my mother. However, I didn't support her. I supported my siblings.

The molestation kept going. But the problem wasn't only the molestation that got to me. It was the mind games he played. That was the real rape. The mind games don't go away. They last forever if you don't get help.

This one time, we were in the shop rite because he was moving, and for some reason, my mom said, "We would help him."

Anyways, we're in shop rite, and he put his hand on my backside. I jumped, and he said, "Look around. No one gives a damn about a little black girl."

So, I looked around, and he was right. No one cared this white man's hand was on this black girl's backside. So, we got to his new house. My family came. He had me sweep the living room. He and my mom went into the bedroom. I went inside the bedroom to sweep inside the room. I saw George getting to14 my mom. My mom jumped up and got dressed. I closed the door and went to my siblings. They came out and acted like nothing happened and so did I. I thought he would leave me alone.

Eventually, he started to ask her questions about me, like "How does it feel when you touch Aisia?" or "How do you feel when you put Aisia in the bathtub."

So, one day, she asked me if he touched me, and I said no. I remember one of the last times I was alone with I was in his car. I had a jean skirt on because my mom was taking us somewhere. Asyou know, the 90's jean skirts were the coolest thing to have. I know I wrote I didn't like dresses, but it was a jean skirt, so I felt like it was just pants. He called me over to the car and to get in. I got in because I thought that because he was in front of his daughter's house, he wouldn't do anything to me. But he did. He went up my skirt. He did the mind games again. He said that he loves skirts because it's easy to have sex. So, I never liked skirts or dresses.

I remember one Saturday, this man walked around the corner of my apartment building. I was outside with my friend Lakeshia.

He came up to my friend and said, "Hi Keshia."

"Hi, Pastor."

When I heard that, I relaxed.

He said, "Are you coming to church tomorrow?"

She said, "Yes."

"I thought tomorrow I could get out of the house, so I asked if I could go."

He said, "Yes, of course."

I was so excited that I forgot to say thank you and just ran upstairs and asked Mom.

She said, "Yes."

So, I went to Keshia's house upstairs to see what she was wearing. I got my clothes for church. I got out of the house for a couple of hours.

"Thank you, Pastor. Whatever I did, it was to get out of the house for at least a couple of hours. It meant survival."

The molestation stopped, and we moved. We moved to Andrew Street, Bayonne, New Jersey. That's where I lost me.

Eventually, D.F.Y.S asked if I had been molested.

I finally said, "Yes. But it wasn't who they believed it was. They thought it was Anthony."

They said, "They were going to protect me, but they didn't."

They left me there. So, I learned how to read people. I learned a lot of things to survive. I was all I had. I learned how to lie really quickly without a tell. This one day, we had just moved to Andrews Street, and we had one bedroom that wasn't full yet. I was home with my siblings, and I had to entertain them. So, I found a key. I don't know where it came from, but we played hot potatoes with it, and I threw it at Essie, and she got cut deep over her eye. At the same time, her dad was walking through the door. I told him Essie was bleeding.

"He asked, "Who did this."

I said, "Anthony."

He would kill me, but he wouldn't hurt Anthony since he was still his little boy. Nobody ever came clean. Since my siblings were aware of what might have transpired, to put it another way, I did what I had to do to live.

"Thank you, little Anthony. I couldn't take living there anymore."

One day, while I was in seventh grade, I recall that several guests from the high school came to speak to my class. They advised us to take it seriously and to report any adult or instructor if someone confides in us with the intention of taking their own life. Just to get help, that was it at that point. And anyhow, who really gave a damn about me, I was going to follow through on it. Even though they were the family, I was bigger than them. That's why I planned to do it tomorrow.

In line at lunchtime, I told two of my friends.

One said, "What?"

The other asked, "Aisia, what are you talking about?"

Before I could say anything, the first one said, "Oh, you're joking." because of what the ladies said yesterday' they both started to laugh.

So, I put my head down and said, "Yes."

They both said, "Good one, Aisia."

I couldn't blame them because I learned how to smile through the pain.

I said to myself, "Yeah, good one, Aisia," walking home, I just thought, "Who would take care of my sibling? I can't do that. They'd have no one. Those four kept me alive for so long. But I knew I couldn't do this anymore."

Chapter 3 - Giving Up

I remember waking up in my room at the house, and my brain said to me, "Aisia Bell left out that window right there. She ran away, and so her siblings won't miss her, we brought you here. Your name is Jessica Campbell."

So, I got up and walked out the door as {Aisia Bell} Jessica Campbell. It was much easier to walk out as Jessica Campbell than it was to be Aisia Bell. Jessica was there because I needed her. I started to think about her back story. She was white and Puerto Rican. Her dad was super rich. She was an open lesbian since she was a little girl. Her birthday was the same as mine. She did not back down to anyone. She had a big family. She was the baby in the family. She was popular. She was blond with blue eyes. She was not sucked up. She was a singer. She was a model. She was a gymnast. And she was my age. She also had powers. Like going invisible when we were sad, speaking only Spanish when we were upset, and literally sitting on fire as we were? The thing was, it was only happening in my head. That was some of her back story.

There were two of them. It was never Aisia Bell for a while; it was her and her brother David, a Robot version of Jessica. Before long, Jessica was by herself. The problem is that Aisia was visible to all. Aisia's voice was heard. Either Iesha or Aisia is my boss. However, I wasn't present. I would mentally go out the window at night. It was she whom the public learned to know. It's weird. After all, this time, she became my best friend because she had my back.

I knew no one could hurt me with her there. Whenever I was alone,

Aisia would go away, and Jessica's day would start. In my mind, she would go to school and get good grades because she was super smart. She would do her job as a singer. She would talk to her girlfriend. She would talk to her dad. His name was Francisco Campbell. That was my favorite place to be because neither was yelling there nor was arguing about me. No one was mad at me, so that's where I wanted to be.

Things were getting bad in school, too. It used to be my happy place, but then it just started to become another place where I got bullied. Church took over that spot as my safe place. No one knew about me, and I was free just to be a kid. It was great. I got to go to church for the Youth group. I was able to go to Sunday school. I was able to go to the prayer meeting. So yes, I lived in church. It was the place where I could be free. Other than church, there were no other places that were safe for me to go. One day in school, I was in eighth grade, my old friends started to pick on me. I was tired of it, so I wrote a letter and gave it to one of them.

It said, "You keep talking about me. Meet me outside and say it to my face."

She said, "OK," assuming that I couldn't fight because I was the quiet one, and that's what she said.

So I was quiet and just waited until lunch. I had the very first of two physical fights in my life. We went to lunch. We went outside. That's when I realized that Bayonne is very races. The girl that I was fighting was white, and me black. So, all the colored girls were in my corner, and all the white girls were in her corner. We fought, and none of the teachers stopped it. The kids said I failed even though the girl fell and left crying. But the most important part was she left me alone. No one ever messed with me again.

"OK, I think I made you all sad enough, so let me tell you all about some of the happy times. When I graduated, my Aunt Betty said she would throw a big party. So, the day after, I waited for her. She never showed up that day, so I went to bed thinking she had forgotten. I never thought that she lied to me. Indeed, I believed that she forgot, perhaps.

The day after, I woke up and went to play with my siblings, outside. While we were playing with our downstairs neighbor, a cab pulled up, and my aunt and cousin got out. It was so exciting. I was so happy. I knew she didn't lie. We went to get food for everyone. Everything I wanted, she got me. It was great. We played and enjoyed the party the whole day.

"Thank you, Aunt Betty. I had a great time. I had great times with my siblings, too."

Like on Christmas Eve, my mom would allow all of us to sleep in the boy's room. We would stay up all night. We didn't go to sleep until the sun came up. Then my mom would come in and say get up. I think there is something out in the living room for you all. We would have so many things to open. My favorite gift of all time was my rollerblades. The best times we had together as a family were when my stepfather was not there. My stepfather was an alcoholic. My mom didn't do anything, not even smoke a cigarette.

My mom made holidays great. She would buy us kids two outfits for Christmas and Easter. For Easter, we had a dress, unfortunately, and a jean outfit. We had nice clothes but nowhere to go. We always decided that the next year we were going to go somewhere or we would have food from a restaurant. I remember one Thanksgiving, I went to my Aunt Betty's house for the holiday. It was so much fun. My cousins and I had so much fun. When I went home, I told my mom everything we did. On Andrew Street, we lived under a lady. She was taken care of by her grandkids. My mom said she could be my father's mother, aka my grandma. The lady never said anything to me. But she was very kind to me. I remember one day after I graduated 8th grade, she called me upstairs. She gave me two balloons and a card with money in it.

I said, "Thank you."

I left her apartment, thankfully. Not becauseof money she gave but because someone thought and cared about me. She went and picked the things up. That made it even better because she thought about me. Although we lived on Andrew St. only for two years, a lot happened there. My uncle came to stay with us for a little while.

My cousin Velda came to live with us. It was so different because she had kids. Whenever I got to see my family, I would get excited. It was so great because they all moved so far away. So, when we got to see them, it was great. Velda had three babies, and she was pregnant with her fourth baby. She was great and always made me feel beautiful. She just would randomly say so many nice things to me. I guess she wanted me to feel like I was loved. That was the thing, no matter how I felt about myself. No matter if I thought I was a weirdo. The Bells never made me feel like that. Even when I thought no one cared if I lived or died, they were right there like, come on, little Iesha, let go and have fun. I love you so much. They are wonderful for that. Velda would take us to places, like the fair and so many places. Even though we were still in Bayonne, it was like we were going to new places. She let me be a child. Not a second mom to my siblings.

"Thank you, cousin."

She made sure we had a good time. Those two years at that apartment were still kind of miner compared to what was to come. Yes, I was depressed. But I was able to handle it well at that time. I was able to smile through the pain. I was able to say ok, my stepfather hates me; ok, my mom doesn't know how to deal with me, but my siblings and the rest of the family love me. I knew that. And I felt that. I knew I was a good big sister. I knew I was a good cousin. I knew I was a good niece. But I didn't like what I looked like. I didn't like who I was. I used to believe that everyone would be better off without me in their lives. The summer before my freshman year of high school, we moved to the last apartment where I lived with my mom. It was 45 east 18th street.

Chapter 4 - I'm Too Broken

So, we moved when I was thirteen. My freshman year was lonely. I was the tallest girl and almost the tallest of all the boys in my grammar school. But in high school, I was surrounded by huge teens. I was so lonely I walked to school alone and back home alone. I didn't talk to anyone there as I had no friends.

Two separate times on my first day of high school, I fell. I arrived home ahead of my siblings at the end of the day. That was quite good. I waited for my siblings while finishing my homework. I had to head straight home because my mom was working at the time. I would feed the kids and myself, and she would prepare our meals. My mother attempted to act more like a mother to me at this point in my life.

But I was already broken. So, I was ok if Mom wanted to hang out or she did not.

Once I was a teenager, I was able to take my sisters with me wherever I went. People I knew stopped recognizing me without two of them; it got that bad. And that's how I liked it because I knew they were safe with me. My first kid was the fourth of them. If they wanted to go to a friend's house, I took them and stayed with them because they were NOT going to go through that which I went. That was not acceptable to me. Protecting them was my birthright. When they wanted to go to play outside, I went with them. Playing outside with them was great, even though Mary didn't play fair enough. I got to be a kid again, and it didn't matter if I was younger than I was. Because if I wanted to be a teen, I had church and school for that. With my sibling, I could be a kid that I never got to be. I would take them everywhere with me, at less Essie and Mary.

The boys stayed home unless I was outside. Then Anthony was allowed to come out with me. But most of the time, just Essie and Mary used to be with them.

During my freshman year, I started working at an after-school program the kids attended. The problem was I was to be broken, and I got sick. This year, 9/11 happened. Everyone thought Bayonne High School would get hit next because it was the next tallest building. I remember where I was. I was leaving gym class. I remember walking in the hallways and hearing the story. I didn't believe it. Why would anyone want to kill Americans? I remember everyone leaving because their parents wanted them home. Because we all thought Bayonne High was next. Before you ask, no, I didn't think I was going home.

My mom wasn't always the one to think she should pick her daughter until and unless when I asked for something, and then she would do her best. That same year, I was in the Girls Glee Club, and we were going to a contest in Hershey Park, Hershey, Pennsylvania. I sold candy wrapping Paper. I sold whatever we had for selling; however, I was still 194 dollars short. My mother promised to come there, and it was the final day I told her. Despite my constant prayers, I never received a call from the front desk. When I arrived at my final Girls Glee Club class, I knew the security guard was getting bored of me because I kept walking down to the front desk.

It was finally time to head out, but I concluded, "I'm not going."

Then the Security guard said, "Aisia Bell."

I turned around, and he handed me an envelope.

He said, "Your mom just dropped this off 25."

I said, "Thank you," and ran up those stairs quickly.

My teacher laughed, saying, "I'll see you in Hershey."

I jumped up and down. After saying my thanks, I let her close the classroom.

I ran home, hugged my mom so hard, and picked her up. She hated when I did that, but she knew I was happy. She brought a lot of things for me to take on the trip with me. We got there and went to our rooms. It was the first time I was in a hotel. And the hotel was in the park. I felt so fancy.

So, two days before the competition, my roommates and I went to the pool. Then we had the air conditioner ON. So naturally, I lost my voice. We went to our teacher, and she said I should drink lemon tea. So, I did, and my voice came back. On the day of the competition we went tothe park the rides were great. Then we went to the competition. The Girls Glee Club came in third place.

The next day, we left and went home. I walked home because my mom thought it was the next day I was coming home. But it was okay because I had to stay in a hotel. I talked about everything there, even to people at church. I didn't care who I spoke to about going on the trip. So, I talked about it.

I got close to some of the teens in the youth group. It was a cool feeling for me as I got out of the house. I had friends. I got to learn about the only Father I had "God." I remember this girl who went to the church with her mom. I befriended her. We used to go to her house for her birthday, Valentine's Day. Anyway, one day, I was done with being at the house, and I was walking to Bayonne High when I kept walking. She lived just past the high school. I knew she was home because she was homeschooled. I also knew she let me in. I wanted to leave, and I wanted to run away. I got to the door of her house, and I stopped. I didn't knock. I didn't move. I just thought, what about Essie, Mary, Anthony and Patrick? Who's going to take care of them? So, I turned around and ran to school. I went to classes. I went to work. I went home, and no one knew I was so close to running away.

I always wanted my siblings not to see and experience any bad moments as much as I did because I tried my hardest not to let them hear the arguing between my mom and their dad. One day, mom went to pick up the kids from the after-school program, and little Anthony asked something that punched me right in the stomach.

He asked, "Is daddy drunk today?"

"Wait a minute. You're just a little kid. You shouldn't have to ask that. Are you also preparing yourself? What am I doing as a big sister? I'm supposed to take all of that from you," I wanted to pick him up and hold him tight.

Instead, I looked at my mom and waited for her answer, but she didn't. Little Anthony knew better than to ask a second time. We all did. I asked my mom if we could go to Al-anon, but we never went. Everything balls down to it because Anthony Fields was always drinking. And he was not a nice or fun drunk. He was a mean one. So, freshman year was very lonely. But my mom started to do more things with me. We would do small things like window shopping and walk down Broadway in Bayonne, and if she had money, we would get a slice of pizza and a drink. I was only allowed juice because my mom didn't give us caffeine until we were 18. That year went by fast.

When summer arrived, my church announced that women would go to camp. I asked my mom if I could go. We teens were supposed to work for it. I said I was supposed to because I never did. A church member always paid for me. That was wonderful. But I always felt like I never worked for it. But I got to go. It was in South Jersey. The ride was beautiful. I was so happy because I wasn't sure if I would go. Even though my mom and I went shopping for my stuff27 to go. She brought me so much. So, anyway, we were in the van, and all I did was look through the window. It was quite fantastic for a girl that never went anywhere other than around Bayonne.

When we finally got there, I knew the country where I wanted to live. It was peaceful. It was big, with trees everywhere and crickets just chirping away; it was great. Then we went into the cabins, and everything was wooden; I loved that décor. It was so big. We bought our 27 stuff inside. We had a mess hall where we made and ate our meals, boys and girls shared a cabin, and a gazebo where we had bible study. It was just wonderful. You could see the stars at night. We made up plays. The boys made up one, and the girls made up one. But the cute thing was that both groups sang the same song at the end of each play. It was Amazing Grace. Soon, it was time to go home and return to reality.

I had so much to tell my mom and siblings when I got home. I didn't stop talking all summer. I knew they were tired of what this person and what that person said or did. But I didn't care. I got to go somewhere. It was so much fun. When I turned 15, I was invited to a super ball party. I went and had fun. After coming back home, I told my mom that my friends called me a lesbian. Which they already knew. That's how I knew you were my real friend. She didn't say anything. I hear Anthony argue from my bed about someone leaving chicken bones somewhere. I ran out the door because I was over it. My mom came out after me, and I told her that I was a lesbian.

She said, "You're just saying that because your friend said it."

I told her, "No. I am a lesbian."

Again, she didn't say anything. We just walked back into that hell hole. I went to bed thinking at least I came out.

Chapter 5 - See You Again Someday Auntie

Well, the beginning of my sophomore year was similar to that of my freshman year. I started to listen to punk rock, Linkin Park, Good Charlotte Simple Plan Blink 182. I also liked Avril Lavigne. But I listened to Marilyn Manson when I was mad. I liked music I could relate to, like "Emotionless" by Good Charlotte. To answer your question, I was called an Oreo. Suppose you don't know what it means. It means something that is black outside and white inside. I didn't understand that just because trying to speak correctly and listening to rock meant I was an Oreo, but that was what people said.

I also liked "Cleaning Out My Closet" by Eminem. The show like Degasses, Boy Meet World, Dawson Creek, Save By the Bell, Full House, Friends, Gilmore Girls, Roseanne, Seven Heaven, and Buffy the Vampire Slayer. I wrote a script for Buffy the Vampire Slayer. I didn't do anything with the script because I wouldn't say I liked the way it ended. You see, I liked songs that meant something that I could relate to. So, these were the songs I listened to while going to school. And those were the shows I loved to watch.

That year, everything kept gradually worsening. It felt like I couldn't get happy. I always felt like everyone would be better off without my absence. I went to school wondering if anyone would ever miss me. There would be arguments about me, about how my dad was not there, or how Anthony took care of me and how he'd done that. I wanted to scream, well, you don't have to.

Christmas of this year made me hate Christmas. My siblings opened their gifts, but I didn't get anything. Well, that was not the sole reason why I was not too fond of Christmas, then. Velda was getting her kids and herself ready to go somewhere. My mom and Anthony were arguing about where we were going to go. Then, my mom went to the bathroom when Anthony choked her. I heard my mom yell at Velda. I jumped up and saw Anthony pull his hand away from my mom's neck. I grabbed the phone from Velda, and then Anthony grabbed the phone from me. I gave him a dead stare and ran outside in the rain.

I called the cops on the pay phone we had on the corner. I told them what happened and that I needed the cops to come to my house. I went back upstairs and thought I had done something good. Velda asked if I had called the cops. I said yes, all happy and proud. When the cops came, I was like, yes, he's out. We don't have to be scared anymore. They were taking him away.

They came to the door and said, "Hello, we got a call from your daughter."

My mom said, "Yeah. She lied."

One of the cops said, "You mean it was a misunderstanding?"

I guess they never heard anyone calling their daughter a liar.

My mom said, "Yes."

They asked if she wanted them to go for a walk.

She said, "Yes."

I was thinking in the background that it would be worse when he returned. That day, I vowed that's not going to be me. After the cops left, we went back to being scared. But I wasn't anymore.

One day, he started to talk about how my dad wasn't doing his job, and I pulled a knife on him. I was going to make him scared of me. I wasn't going to be weak anymore. I started to say whatever was on my mind, and I didn't care about anyone's feelings, as if none cared about mine.

One day, My Aunt Carol was sick. I didn't know how ill she was. When I came home, my mom told me to put my book bag down and said we were going to my cousin John Jr.'s house. So we got the kids and went to John Jr.'s house. John Jr. is the person I have called my big brother since I was a little girl. He had three siblings of his own. His little brother Winfield and I used to argue about whose big brother John Jr. was. Velda and Veda were their sisters. Anyway, we went there, hung out, and chilled. Whenever you're with Winfield, you will have a good time. Eventually, we had to go home. So, we went into Auntie's room and said our goodbyes.

I said, "Bye, and I love you."

She said, "Bye, Iesha," and we left.

Although I said bye, I believed that was not bye, and it was not the last time I saw her.

A few days after I came home from school, my mom said, "Aisia, put your book bag down."

I knew what that meant. I went back to when I lost grandma. This time, I knew what that meant. We went to John's house again, and everyone was there, and I was like a robot that time. My mom was about to pass out, and I held her up. But what I remember the most was Winfield falling on her grave. He was one of her kids. Her kids were John Jr., Velda, Winfield, and Veda. When I saw him fall out, I just started to pray for all her kids. After that, we went to John's house and had a meal.

We returned home, but I wasn't there anymore. I wanted to die too. I couldn't fight anymore. My Auntie Betty also came to live with us. Again, I didn't understand how someone from a big family could still feel lonely. There were so many people in the house, but no one could know what I thought or felt. No one knew how much I was done. They didn't even know how deeply I was hurt. I didn't think there was a way out of my thinking. But I knew I had to smile through the pain, and I knew how to put a smile on the face.

When people asked how my day was, I would reply, 'It was fine' because I didn't know whether they really wanted to know or merely asked to comply with the formality. I always wished I could read people's minds. Because then I would know what they really meant and said. If they really liked me. That's why I started to read people. This year was crazy because I started to have seizures again. I had them as a child, but they returned when I turned 15.

Chapter 6 - The K.A.R.E House

My morning routine consisted of getting up earlier, washing my face, and brushing my teeth. I would put on some clothes. I would get my sweater. Since I was not fond of jackets or coats, I used sweaters. Then, I would leave and walk to school the same way every day. I would get breakfast there and then go to my classes. Then, I would hurry up and get my little cousin; we would walk home. I would do my homework and watch TV for the rest of the day. At night, my mom would want to talk to me about sex. She thought I was having sex. She thought I was going to be like her. I would have to stand in her doorway and listen to her. If I blinked my eyes, she would think I was rolling my eyes. All I wanted to do was go to bed.

One day, while my cousin and I were walking home, I found 40 dollars. I told my cousin I would give him a dollar if he were good. So, we went home, and when his mom came home, he told her he found the money, and I promised to give him the money. I told her the truth. She told me I didn't have to give him the dollar and gave me 40 more dollars. I had 80 dollars, the most I had in my pocket. I waited for my mom to take me to the shop right. I got some snacks. I got 33 white cranberry juice and black olives. That is what I love to eat.

One day, I wrote a little book called, "Walk in My Shoes," I was always a writer.

I wrote every time I had a lot of feelings about something. And I didn't know how to express it. But it wasn't always bad. To this day, my brother Anthony talks about the stories I wrote for them. After writing that book, I went to the bathroom, grabbed a handful of medication, and took it to school. My mom didn't have a gun, so I thought I could die from an overdose because that is what you hear in Dare. Dare was a group that the firefighters had for kids to learn about drugs and how just to say no. So, we learned that kids were dying from taking meds from their parent's medicine cabinet. So, I went to school and took it to the water fountain. It didn't work.

Two days later, I wrote a suicidal note. I had it in my pocket. It felt out in English class. I didn't notice. I went to my last class. I went to pick up my cousin, and we went home. That day, I decided to go the back way. When we got home, my Aunt Betty was cleaning up. That was strange for me because she was at home. She was usually at work at this time. Some of us went in, and my aunt told my cousin to go and play in the boys' room.

She said that my school had come to the house and they found my letter. She asked if I really wanted to die.

I lied and said, "No, auntie."Because how could I tell her? Yes, I didn't want to be here anymore. That I hate living here. That I hate me.

I didn't know how to say all these things to her. I couldn't believe it fell out of my pocket. So, when she wasn't looking, I checked, and it was gone. She said they went to get my mom and were coming back for me. She called them, and they said they were coming and to keep me there. She told me to tell them that it was a joke.

I said, "OK."

They came upstairs and got me. I left with them. They kept trying to get me to talk. All I could think about was a couple of things, like lying to my aunt. My mom then knew how I really felt. And I was supposed to protect her. And the last part was I told the secret. I got back to school, and my mom was crying. I went into the office, and my mom rubbed my back. I saw my teacher come in with my letter. We talked about the letter.

They asked if I really felt like that, and I finally said, "Yes."

After I said that, I looked at my mom, and she couldn't even look at me.

They said, "We are going to take Aisia to the hospital."

They took my mom and me to the emergency room. We stay there overnight. My mom kept trying to get me to smile. But all I could think about was those same three things. My aunt Betty called.

The nurse said, "Iesha, we don't have an Iesha Bell."

Then she asked if they had any Bells teen that came in with their mom. The nurse came in and said Betty Bell was on the phone.

My mom got up, and I heard her say, "Yeah, she is staying."

My Aunt Betty must have said, I thought she said, "She didn't feel like that."

My mom said, "I know, but she said she did."

I was like, "I know. I lied to your auntie."

"Sorry for lying, Auntie Betty. I love you."

From Bayonne Hospital, I went to St. Mary's Hospital. My mom and I went upstairs there, and then she had to leave. And all I could think was who was going to protect her. And I lied to my aunt. ThereWe, teens and preteens, had a group to help us. The youngest was five. He jumped out of the window in school. He was five, really. I met this one gay guy who was my age, and he had aids. That was like wow. And he told everyone.

We went to the group to talk about what was bothering us. I felt one group was the best because the counselor showed she cared. The boy told the story about how he got aids. This one girl named Meagan told the story about both of her parents dying in the same week, and I told the story about Anthony coking my mom on Christmas. I guess the counselor couldn't hold it in anymore because she started to cry after I was done. It was she and a male counselor in the room. The male counselor hugged her.

I didn't know how the other person felt about that, but I just wanted to thank her because that was the first time I had said it to anyone since the police officers. Her crying made me feel like she cared about what we went through. So, we went to a group to talk to kids our age. I got to call my mom and siblings. We had community meetings that were important later. In community meetings, we discussed what or who we had a problem with. It was the time we just uttered what was on our mind. We had to have a voice. I had a voice. I was diagnosed with major depression.

My time was up there, and I went home. I thought that was that I'd take these meds and would be happy. That is not how life works. It is not a science. It's more of pass and fail. But it wasn't always mental health. I also went to the hospital for seizures. One Day, I went to the Hospital and got so many visitors. One was my cousin Velda. The other ones were my youth group. They were all there to see me. That was the best moment when they came around the corner. And I saw them. Another time, I went to the hospital because I was allergic to the medicine that they gave me for the seizures. That day was crazy because I woke up late to go to school and had to rush. I walked out of my bedroom to get ready when

Velda said to my mom, "Rachel, she can't go to school."

Velda said, "Go and look at your face."

I looked in the mirror and thought someone had eaten me, and I was looking through their eyes.

I went home, and things seemed to get better. My mom was working, and where she was working, they sold all kinds of stuff. She told them about me being depressed, and I loved to read. They just happened to have this book called "A Lost Boy" by David Pelzer. That was what I was going to do. I was going to write for that next teen. I was going to write my story for whoever needed to hear it. I didn't care what people thought. His book was so powerful. It was a page-turner. When I reached the end, I saw it was his second book. I read that book repeatedly.

I knew I wanted to inspire someone. I knew I wanted to tell someone that things get better, just not at that time. Because I didn't see a way out YET, but I knew if I didn't end my life, I was going to write my story. I eventually got the other books. I read them all. I just loved his writing.

I went back and forth from the hospital four times in two months. Until the doctor said that I was going to this group home called the

Kare house. I don't know what it stands for. I had a fit. Not because I finally leaving the house but because that doctor didn't know or understand that I didn't trust Anthony. Who was going to protect my family? They put me in a quiet room. I wrote a paper about how I felt my mom gave up on me, and I called my mom and told her she cried, and that's the last time I told her how she made me feel. Because I make my mom cry, I'm no better than Anthony.

All I ever wanted was for my mom to love me. Everything I would ever do was to show my mom that I was better than her. I never repeated anything. She was crying because of me.

She used to say, "It's me and you against the world, kid."

I believe that, "Then why am I making her cry?"

I used to cry every time I heard the song You Are My Sunshine. Because my mom sang it to me, I didn't understand why Anthony had to be there. I got off the phone and grew up. I went to the Kare house two days later.

When I got there, I got to see Meagan again from the hospital. I met a couple of more teens. The staff was great. I had a route. We went somewhere every day. We had to eat breakfast every morning. I wouldn't say I liked that because I disliked breakfast. We would have a morning meeting. We would have a community meeting. We would go to school, and then we would go to this other place. We never just stood still. On Wednesdays, the boys or the girls would go food shopping each week. That was different for me. We were buying so much food for one week. Wow ok. Anyways, whichever group that went the other would put it away. I like putting it in because I could organize the pantry. One of the staff always taught us how to cook from scratch. We cook so many things. Meagan Marissa was my roommate at first. After months of being there, I got to see my mom. Then, I went on weekend trips home.

The weekend trips home were different, but they were familiar at the same time. My mom and I got closer. We were mother and daughter. I got to talk to my Aunt Rose on the phone. I got to see my siblings. I didn't stay in my room all day, every day. We went outside. It felt like a family. I felt like I was part of the family. I would go back to the Kare house.

One day, Meagan Morrow came. I didn't know at that time, but she was going to be my best friend, and not just at that time. Love you, Meagan. So yes, there were two Meagan. Meagan Ma. And Meagan Mo. Meagan Mo. was my second roommate. And wow, she made my time there so much better. She was Irish, so she loved the green care bear. So, one weekend home, I went with my mom window shopping when I saw this toe ring that was the color of the Irish flag, and I wanted to get it for her.

Hold on before you say anything. That was the style back then. It was great being Meagan Morrow's roommate. She used to trap these moths with tape and stick it to this book. She helped me write the song "Emotionless" by Good Charlotte on paper so I could send it to my dad. She was younger than me, but she knew a lot. Maybe because my head was always in a book, I remember how she taught me to say her last name.

She said, "It's Morrow, like tomorrow."

That always made me laugh. I remember her telling me she liked, liked me. I told her I liked her too, but she didn't believe me.

I remember her wanting to jump out the window one summer when the lights went out. She wanted to go looting. She was the bad girl. At that time, she thought I was so innocent. We grew so close that even when I left, I would call her. She made me feel like I wasn't weird or different. She took me as I was. I never had to read her. She never made me wish I could read her mind to know how she really felt about me. She never bit her tongue, so I knew she meant what she said. Love you, Meagan Mo.

I started there for a year. I went in at 16, and I left at 17. The counselors didn't know if they were going to send me back home or to independent living. But the D.Y.S.F. worker my mom had so long ago told them I would do better at home. So, they sent me home. When I got home, we had a community meeting. My mother asked us to go around the room what we wanted, and my brother Anthony said he didn't want me to leave again. I wish I could've done that.

Chapter 7 - Becoming An Adult

I left the Kare House and went home. I went back to Bayonne High School. However, the high school I went to during the time I went to did not have credits, so I had to redo my sophomore year. Even today, whenever I go to Bayonne High School for my transcripts, it says 10, 10, 11, 12. So it's like my freshmen year didn't happen. Talk about feeling invisible. I felt like I worked so hard in school for nothing. When I went back, I had to go to classes in the basement that didn't go around.

It was extremely special ed. So, we went to the gym by ourselves. We went to lunch by ourselves. We didn't join the rest of the high school. The only times I got to see other people were Spanish class and math class. I got to take math class out of the class because of the math I already knew. There was this girl who was half black and half white, and she was very racist against black people. She lived with her dad, and he was racist against black people. She used to tell too many jokes, so I put gum in her hair one day. I walked up behind her, put the gum on, and walked away. She needed to realize she was black, too. I stayed there for a year.

I eventually went back to my regular classes. I was in 11 grade finally. I turned 18 in the 11 grade. That really stunk. Everyone in my class was two years younger. I went back to the Girls Glee Club. I didn't have friends that year. I really was alone. So, I got depressed again. I wondered if I died, would anyone care? I would walk around Broadway and wonder if anyone cared about me. I went back to the hospital again. I went into the adult psych ward. There, I met a guy named Mike. He was bisexual. He was in the psych ward, too. He understood what I was going through. So, I thought it was a good idea to be his girlfriend when he asked me to be. I thought my mom would be happy because he was a guy.

He was 27, and I was 18. But my mom wasn't happy with him. She didn't think he was right for me. Because we both had mental health issues, he came to my mom's house a couple of times to pick me up. My mom was always cordial with him. But I know when she doesn't like someone. We would go to his mom's house. He lived there. Or we could go to the mall. He didn't like the fact that he was overweight. So, he was ever insecure about it.

One time, Mike picked me up from my mom's house. We went to the mall and hung out. He had weak knees, so he fell and couldn't get up. We called the ambulance. We went to the hospital. I called my mom to keep her updated. She was fine with me being the at first, but then it started to get late, so she was not having it. She told me to get my backside home. So, I told him, and he cried and said I was abandoning him. I don't do well with crying. But I told him I had to leave.

I got a light rail ticket from him and left. I didn't want to leave because that was not right. I didn't think it was cool to leave someone that needed me. I got on the first train that came, not knowing where it was going. The train went to Westside Avenue in Jersey City. I went out of the train and didn't know where I was. Luckily, I forgot to give Mike his cell phone back. So, I called my mom. I told her that I was stuck in Jersey City.

She said, "OK," she said to stay where I was, and she would call a cab to get me. I got in the cab and went home.

The next day I went to Mike's house and gave him his phone back. That was whenwe broke up because I didn't stay with him. I went home. I went into my room and cried, not because we broke up but because I thought I was doing the right thing by dating a guy. Like, isn't that want you wanted? He called and bragged me to return to him, but I just said we couldn't date anymore. He started to cry again. I felt like a jerk. After Mike, I didn't go out with anyone. I was just focused on school.

After I finished the Kare house, two people came to the house. They were from two different programs. I don't remember the names of the programs. But one got me into a program like Big Brother and an extensive sister program. The other one had little groups we could go to as a family. We got to learn how to make bread from starch. It was cool to know. We went there on Saturdays to make bread. Then, the teens would go to a group after school one day of the week. We would hangout, talk with each other, and have dinner. We would talk about what was bothering us as teens and what we were going through. And all the stuff like that. I went to that group for two years. Last year I went there with Essie. That was fun because we got to hang out.

One day, while I was there, one of the guys asked when I knew I was gay. I was taken aback, but I answered by saying I was eight and had a crush on my best friend. Essie never said anything. She just went with everything and said nothing. She was the greatest for that. I was going to tell them, "As in my siblings," but not like that. I did not know how to and didn't know what I would say to them.

When we left, I said, "Yeah, I'm a lesbian, and Mommy knows already. But don't tell Mommy that she knew."

She said, "OK," and she didn't.

My mom didn't know she knew until we got older.

"I love you, Essie. You're a real one."

Chapter 8 - Senior Year

Senior year was the best year. It was wonderful. I had an English teacher that was the best. Her name was Mrs. Bonner. She made my senior year great. My home room was next to one of my best friend's homerooms. Her name was Diana. She was from my grammar school too. We would meet before homeroom and during Girl's glee Club. We would walk to the bus stop together. She would get on the bus, and I *would walk home. Yes, I would walk home by myself,* but it felt different.

Mrs. Bonner would let me eat lunch in her classroom. I would be able to get to listen to relaxing music. I don't know how it started, but That's how it was. Mrs. Bonner paid for everything that I needed for my senior year. She would give me money for lunch. I got a free lunch, but I like the chicken wrap and a Gatorade. So, when I would get the money, it would be great. Mrs. Bonner helped me so much. I also had a friend in her class; her name was Anna. Anna and Diana were friends too. I always felt like the third wheel, but I guess there was my friend at that time. In gym class, I met two girls. One of the girls invited me to a lgbt meeting for teens. It happened every Friday.

I told my mom, and she said, "No way, no how."

I was not going, but they were my friends. I got to hang out with people in school for the first time and got to say I had friends.

I had so much fun doing everything for senior year. I went to senior day. For some reason, we didn't go to the pool that year. The seniors went to the pool every other year, but not that year. I don't remember why. But the senior day was in our high school. It was great, hot but great. I got to go to prom. Prom was great. My mom still has a picture of me in a very pink dress. But yeah, Mrs. Bonner not only brought the dress, but she also took my mom and me to get it. I got my hair done and everything. I had jewelry on, and that felt so good. Mrs. Bonner took my mom and me to the high school like that was cool.

When I got to the gym, I noticed that Anna and Susan were there. Yes, the very same Susan from when I was nine. I was like, what in the world?

She said she went to prom with some guy who was a senior. But she hung out with Anna and me because we were having fun. But I let her because I wanted her to know her father didn't break me that bad. No, I didn't bring it up because if you remember, in the begin, I said I woke up to my hand on her backside and his hand on mine, so I think he did something to her too. Besides that, it was the first time I'd seen it.

What was I supposed to say?"Oh, how your is a child molester of a father."

Yeah, I don't think so. So, we hung out, danced, and we had fun.

I also got to hang out with the two girls from the gym. The dance floor was great. I thought I was fancy because I was there. Mrs. Bonner picked me up after we got back to Bayonne high school. Then, It was graduation. That was great; my mom and siblings snuck in. I heard them from the front. They yelled so loud it was nice. We went home, and I got ready to go to project graduation. Project graduation is what my high school called the party after graduation. You would return to school in the evening, and we would be taken to some private hotel. We only knew that we should bring a bathing suit and a towel. We stay up all night. I got an artist to draw a picture of a cartoon of me working as a chef on a cruise ship. But I didn't know what I wanted to do for a living. I did know I wanted to travel. But I didn't know what I wanted to be. I didn't even know who I was. We had two more days after high school. I left school not knowing what to do.

Chapter 9 - Leaving My Mom's House

That summer was weird. I know I was already an adult, but it's an odd feeling when you're not attending school in September.

I went to church camp for the last time. Essie went for her first time. That was fun for me Because I got to show her everything. She did not like the bugs. She was a girly girl when it came to that. We had bags full because our mom loves to pack bags over. During the summer, I started to go to a day group. It was for adults who had mental health issues. I would walk around Broadway with my mom. She wanted me to get a job. I told her we went to Social Security so I could get SSI. So, I didn't understand why I would get a job while trying to earn income.

Essie graduated 8th grade when I graduated 12th grade. So, she was going into freshman year. I didn't get to see her first day. I didn't get to hear about it either. One day, Anna asked if I could spend a night at her mom's house.

I said, "Sure."

I left thinking I would spend one or two days there and return home until I got my apartment.

The next day, I returned to my mom's house, and she packed my stuff in a garbage bag. She said, "Do you want to see if you can stay with your friend?"

I didn't fight her. I didn't ask where I would go; I just took my bag, put a smile on my face, and said, "OK."

I walked back out the door and left my mom's house. When I left her house, I was 19, Essie was 14, Mary was 13, Anthony was 12, and Patrick was 11. They were all in or finished high school when I finally saw them again. I walked out that door, thinking what I was going to do. Anna's mom's name was Margarita, and her stepdad's was Arthur. I knew she smoked on the back porch. So, I went to the back porch, but she wasn't there. I got up the nerves to knock on the door. She saw me with my clothes in a black garbage bag. I told her what happened and waited for her answer, which seemed forever.

She looked at me and said, "Anna was not here anymore. She moved in with her boyfriend."

I said, "OK," and I was about to turn around when she did not come in.

"You stay here."

"Thank you, Margarita. I love you, and I know you watch over me."

I'm finally writing my book. I walk into the house. I got to stay in Anna's old room for a little. Margarita and I would sit on the porch in the back yard. I would go to the day care in the morning.

One day, Margarita and I were in the backyard. She was smoking a cigarette, and she gave me one. She said it would relax me.

So, I said, "Sure," and took my first cigarette.

Yes, I had my first cigarette at 19. Margarette took me to Social Security for SSI. Margarette would tell me about her life, and I would tell her about mine, at least what has happened to me so far. Soon, Arthur's mom came from Panama. I don't think she liked me. I learned to read people I knew when I wasn't wanted. So, I was in and out of the hospital. Margarita and Arthur were very nice, but I knew I couldn't stay there.

The last time I went to the hospital, they called my mom. She said that she had the other kids to worry about. They called Margarita, and they said no. so I didn't have a place to go. So, while people my age were concerned about a test, I was worried about where I would go. The case manager told me to give up my rights so I could be committed to the hospital because they didn't have a place for me to go. So, I did. Please hang on tight because the next two years werea whirlwind. I did think my mom would come and see me before I left, but she never did.

Mommy was in Bayonne with no car. So, she couldn't get anywhere else. I left Bayonne Hospital and went to one in Secaucus. I stayed there twice. The first time was a couple of months ago. Then I went to some place in south Jersey. I remained there for about five months. There, I had two girlfriends. I didn't care. I broke one girl's heart because no one cared about mine. The second girl had a husband and a son. I didn't care. She started to catch feelings. I wasn't having that. She was a trophy to me. Me and some other guy liked her. She chose me, and that was that.

I won. I know, I know, immature. I didn't want anyone getting close to me. I didn't think I deserved that. I was a loser who lived in the hospital. Like I never got to see outside. I was in prison.

I said, "I was in a hospital for two years. It could have been more like three. I'm not sure. I left that hospital and went to a boarding home/ hospital. Then, I went to someplace that made those spoons, knives, and napkin kits. I have lived there for a little while. Then, I went to another group home in Atlantic City. I stay there for a couple of days. Then I went back to Secaucus."

I stayed there for almost a year. If I say I lived somewhere, ask me if it was in the hospital. I signed one paper that was supposed to help me, but I just got bounced around. The last time I was in Secaucus, I met some lovely people. The nurses and doctor never understood why I was so depressed. Well, sir, maybe it's because I'm 21 and live in the hospital. I also met this one girl who had some problems with me. We had breakfast, and she said something about my mom. I was not having that, so I told her to shut up. She pushed the table. I moved it back, and she got up and pushed it harder. It cut the bottom of my foot so bad I need stitches. I required stitches twice. The doctor put me on suicide watch. Because of the fight, I didn't hit her. After that, I gave up.

I didn't think I would ever get out of the hospital. I started to believe I was worthless. I didn't think anyone cared. And if you're wondering if my mom knew where I was. Well, the answer is yes, I called her. I always wonder if she thought I left and then went back in. But she never called or showed up. It was just me in there. On holidays and birthdays, every day, it was just me. I finally got out. I went into a boarder home in East Orange. There, I met Emma. I thought she was a friend. But I was a check. I got out of the hospital because Social Security finally gave me SSI, so I had income.

After three years, I hated everyone and everything. I didn't care about my life or anyone else. I was left in the hospital for three or more years with no one in my family caring if I was death or alive. Emma convinced me to move in with her, and we got a rooming house. I didn't know, but Emma was using crack. She loved it when we did it together. I did it a couple of times because who cares what I did? When I had money, Emma was nice to me. She never called me her girlfriend. So, I guess I was just her special friend. We used to go to her dad's house and see her son. I would lay on the floor at night and wonder what happened to me. I would pray for God to take me away. I stayed with Emma for another maybe three months.

One day, I was done with my life. I had been kicked so much that I was done. I got high with Emma and took an overdoes. I told Emma goodbye. I told her that I smoked and took all my meds. She thought I was lying. I told her I wasn't. And I went to sleep. I woke up in the hospital. I was in the ICU. The doctors said I died twice on the table.

And all I could think was, "Why didn't you leave me there?"

The cops came into my room to get me to say Emma gave me something.

I said, "No."

She didn't and stuck with that. The next day, I was discharged. I thought I was going to the psych ward, But I just went home. I got there, and Emma was gone. I was there for five minutes because of where I would go. Then I got my stuff and left the rooming house.

"Thank you, Emma, because without you calling 911, I wouldn't be here. You saved my life."

I met this guy through Emma. He knew I was a lesbian. But he also knew that I needed a place to live. He had a girlfriend, so he told her I was his cousin. I learned that to get what I needed or wanted, I had to give men what they wanted. I realized that was all I was suitable for. I eventually got tired, and I went back to the hospital. But after the times with Emma, I didn't do crack again.

Chapter 10 - Meeting My Future Family

I was in the hospital for about a month when this lady came to talk to me. Her name was Tawana Hunter. She came and told me what I wanted to hear. I had a place to go once I got out of the hospital. So, I got out of the hospital.

The moment I got there, a lady who lived there pulled me to the side and said, "Whatever Tawana said, she lied. She is not going to give you that amount of money," she told me Tawana lied about everything.

That's okay. I was always being lied to. The lady was my roommate and didn't like me because I did everything wrong. I didn't know how to clean. I snored when I was on my back. But if I was on my side, I didn't. She would poke me with a stick. She would send me to the store for drug paraphernalia, and she would give me a couple of dollars to go to the store for her because I was not being paid.

No, the store didn't sell drugs, but you buy somethings there that help you smoke crack. She used to brag about what she had me do. She was an older woman. Not a couple of years older than me. Older like she had kids my age. One day, I got sick and tired of it, and I told her to leave me alone. She tried to fright me, and I pushed her. I kicked her, and she left me alone. Tawana got a more prominent place up the block, so we all moved up there. I finally got my room.

I don't know if she complained about me so much, but I got my room. My old roommate had me go and get her drugs for her. And she gave me dope. I used that twice; that's it. I was depressed, and I wound up in the hospital again. When I came out and went home, this lady was on the pouch and had this 10-month-old girl with her. The lady was named Stacy, and the little girl was her baby, Ella. Stacy said I did not belong at her sister's boarding home from that first day. I thought maybe she saw me. Perhaps I would finally be ok.

So, Stacy said she would get her place, and I could live with her, Ella Stacy's son's girlfriend, son, and boyfriend. Stacy had my back from the first time I met her. While she was there, I went into the hospital, and the doctors saw dope in my blood. So, the doctor sends me to a facility in Pennsylvania. They got me a bus ticket there. I stay there for three days. They said that I didn't need to be there. I told them if I went back, I was going to die, but they didn't care. So, I got on a bus back to Newark, New Jersey. When I got there, I returned to the boarding home.

When I got to the house, it was Ella's first birthday. I stayed there for about another month. Then Stacy and Iall moved to Stacy's boyfriend's bedroom apartment. That's when I learned the phrase get in where you fit in. We started there in about another month. Then we move into a three-bed apartment. I shared a room with Ella. That was ok because I had a room. Stacy saw me, and she gave me a room. When we moved, It was on New Year's Eve.

I cashed my check, and I had my whole check. I went into Stacy's room and asked her what I owed her. She said I didn't owe her anything. So, I went to go to my mom's house. Yes, I was free. I was not in the hospital or the boarding home, so I got up and left to see my siblings. Before I got on the bus, I went to this store. They had little wrestling men, so I got it for Patrick. I got on the bus and went to Penn Station. I took the train to Journal Square. From Journal Square, I took bus # 10 and got to Bayonne. I got off on 21st Street and walked down to 18th Avenue E.

I walked into the building and up the stairs to the first floor. I knocked on the door.

My mom opened it up and said, "Aisia, what are you doing here?"

I said, "I wanted to see you guys."

She let me in, and I gave Patrick his gift. Essie ran up and hugged me. Mary and Patrick hugged me, too. I had to force Anthony to hug me. I gave them each a hundred dollars Because I didn't want them to feel left out. I gave Mommy some money, too. Then I went to take a shower. That felt so weird because I didn't live there anymore.

My mom had my room the same as when I was a kid. Like she was waiting until I came home, I didn't tell them what I went through. I didn't tell them that I died. I was home. I got to see my family. My family. That was the thing I lived with so many people. I finally got to see my family. I never thought I was going to see them again. I spun two nights there. Yes, that's right, I said I spun two nights. We went on Broadway. But this time, I wasn't window shopping but buying stuff. I loved the feeling of buying things for them.

Then my mom asked if I was going back home.

Again, I put a smile on my face and said, "Yeah, ok."

I left broke. I went back to the house and walked into my room.

Stacy asked if I had the money her boyfriend gave me to get an I.D., and I told her the truth. No, I didn't. She made a notice, and I felt like I was nothing.

I don't know what I expected, but I didn't think two days was enough time for my siblings.

I said, "I know when I'm not wanted. I also know that you must pay where you stay," so I got up and walked out.

My mom gave me some clothes, so I took what she gave me and left. I didn't know where I was going to go. But I thought maybe if I got to Bayonne, I could go to my Pastor, who could help me. As I walked back to Penn Station, Stacy came running out and called me.

She said, "Girl where you are going."

I told her I didn't know.

She said, "Girl, get back in the house, making me run out here for you."

"Thank you, Stacy, you really made me feel wanted. I really felt like someone cared if I lived or died."

After that day, Stacy had me. Everything she said was like gold. She told me she had a nephew for me. She said I would be good for him. And before you asked, she knew I liked girls.

Living with Stacy in the beginning was cool and great. All I did was listen to everything she said. I believed her and argued with anyone who said she was wrong. One day, she said she would return to Sumter, South Carolina. She said she would find a house there because it was cheaper.

I Never went anywhere that wasn't in New Jersey, so I was excited to go. She left with Ella and her son's girlfriend. She returned after a few weeks, saying that her son's girlfriend played her. She said that when they got to Sumter, the girl left with the girl's mother and left her at the train station. All the girls planned it out, and all she wanted to do was use Stacy to get back there. Stacy said she had to walk to her mom's house. She also said she came back for her son and me. Her son didn't want to go back there. But I did. So, a couple of days later, Stacy, Ella, and I got on a bus. I never told my mom I left. I didn't think she would care anyway. I just left.

We got to Sumter about 18 or 19 hours later. I don't know how long it was. I was fine with that because I love long car trips. If I were on a short trip, I would feel like I could have walked there. Anyway, we got there, and Stacy's mother came to pick us up so we could go to Social Security so I could get my SSI transferred over to Sumter. At that time, I needed a Payee. So, Stacy's mom said she would be my payee. Then we went to her mom's house, where I met Stacy's sister Cassandra.

As soon as she said that name, I thought about the Kare house because there was a girl named Cassandra, and we called her Cassie. So, I asked her if she went by Cassie. She said sometimes. Stacy told her to stop lying. She said some people called me that. I just laughed. Because I thought it was nice to see siblings joking. I missed mine.

Once we got there, a lot of the family came. It was Stacy's little nephews. Not just the one she told me about. Her sister and brother. His kids. They were hanging out in the living room. Her brother was my kid's future grandfather. His name was Lloyd, but everyone called him by his middle name Andre. Stacy's mom's name was Emma. It was so many families who came that first day I got tried. Mrs. Emma told me I could lie in her room, so I did. I was done for the day. I took a shower, changed my clothes, and went to bed.

Chapter 11 - Meeting My Kids' Father

My future kid's dad's name was John. But everyone called him Jay. I saw Jay the first day, but. I got to talk to him the next day. We talked, and he went back to his parents' house. When he came back, he had his clothes in a garbage bag. When I saw that, I went back to when I left my mom's house. He said his parents kicked him out. I found out later that was not true. But that's what he said so that's what I believed. So, we were talking, and he said he could move in with his cousin. I told him Stacy and I were getting a house. Why doesn't he move in with us? He said he could do that. He said he lived with Stacy before.

Let me tell you all that I did not know all the drama that came with this family. But anyway, he said he would have to ask her. I said I would ask. That day, we went to the Salvation Army. I got Jay a whole new wardrobe. The Salvation Army had a book section. I was more interested in their books; it was a bag of books for a dollar. I jumped on that deal. Then we went to the mall. Stacy and I got some clothes from there. I brought Mrs. Emma some clothes too. We went back to Mrs. Emma's house.

Stacy, Ella, and I would sleep in one bed at bedtime. We slept in a room that had wooden walls. I loved it because it reminded me of the church camp. I love that look. Anyway, one day, we were all asleep when I woke up to Stacy yelling at Aisia to get off her. When I got up, I was laying on Ella like she was a pillow. We both were knocked out. So, I guess I lift my head high enough so she can crawl under my head. I don't know how, but it happened. We all started laughing.

One day, we went to welfare, where everything was in one building. So, we were on the first floor, which had WIC and the free clinic. We went to the clinic for Ella. We passed this lady and her baby. I, of course, saw the baby.

Jay said, "Hi."

The lady said, "Hi."

I didn't think anything of that because I learned that everyone says hi to everyone in the South.

So, I kept walking when Stacy said to Jay, "Are you going to say hi to your mom?"

I thought his mother, like these two, acted like they were strangers. I didn't understand that because no matter what I went through with my mom, I wouldn't act like I didn't know her. Now, that's just disrespectful. So, I looked at him and got up.

I walked up to her, put my hand out, and said, "Hi, my name is Aisia, and it's nice to meet you."

She said hi, but she gave 'the I don't like you look.' I asked how old her baby was she said 3. I said bye to her, and I said bye to the baby. Then I walked back to where I was. Again, I did not know the drama that the family came with. But I was starting to see what I got myself into. We left there and didn't even talk about what happened. Soon, I got to hear about how bad that lady was. How much of a bad mother she was. I was thinking, but she was at the clinic with her son.

She was doing what she had to do.

One day, Jay's dad came by with Jay's brothers. They were so small. His brothers' names are Kevin, Tony, and Kenneth. Kenneth was the baby that I saw with their mom. They came for a little barbecue. It was fun. But that was when I found out Jay never called his siblings. Like, man, you're their big brother. I didn't understand. I didn't call my siblings either don't get me wrong. But if I could've had. We lived there for about a year. It was a nice home. But then I started to get depressed again. Jay and I were arguing so much because I'm a lesbian. And what doesn't a lesbian want to do with a guy? That's right, I didn't want to sleep with him. It was disgusting. He was a guy. I had to think of two girls like Allison Hannigan, Eliza Dushku, and other famous women. I did that whenever I felt bad enough to do something with him. He would tell everybody about our bedroom time together. He told everyone it was terrible. I didn't care what he said because I didn't want to do it anyway. He was a guy.

You're probably wondering why I didn't just break up with him and didn't sleep with another man. To answer the first one, I felt bad for him because he said he had no one, and I know the feeling of not having anyone. And to answer the second one, yes, I slept with other men, but it was out of necessity, not that I liked them or that I wanted them to be my boyfriend. So, we would argue a lot. So, of course, I went back to the hospital because I felt like everything was my fault. When I got out, Stacy decided she was done with the South, and Jay didn't remember New Jersey. So, we decided to move back. But we had a party before we left, and Jay's mom came. Jay's mom's name was Shanta. I wanted her to like me so much. I ran out of the house to see her. We were walking towards the back of the house, and she asked me if Jay and I were using protection. I told her sometimes.

I didn't tell her we were not always doing that because I didn't like men.

She said, "You're going to be pregnant in no time."

I said, "No," but what I was thinking was that I wanted a baby.

I helped raise my siblings I know how to care for a baby. I always wanted to be a mother. Stacy's boyfriend at that time was still in Newark. So, he got us an apartment. He came to Sumter and got us. His income came from something bad at that time. He sold weed. He also smoked weed. What we didn't know was that he was smoking more than he was selling. So, we left with him. We moved into our place. Stacy and I got it closer. We were already close, though. I remember Stacy sitting on the floor of her bedroom on her birthday. And she was crying sing Happy Birthday to me. She was rocking back and forth. I went in there and held her, and we just sat in silence. I didn't understand why she didn't leave him. But I didn't ask her that.

One day, we went to Tawana's boarding home. It felt different. I was going back to the place I lived. I was going to see my aunt. At this time, I started to call Jay's aunt Auntie, Jay's grandma. That one hurt because I know and love my grandma. So, I was going to my aunt's place. When we got there, I saw the girl who cut me on my foot in the hospital.

She said, "Aisia, how are you doing?"

"If you don't get out of my face," I gave her a look like a girl.

I asked Stacy if we could go.

She said, "Yeah."

I started to feel weird soon after that. I felt something kick me in my stomach. I told Stacy she would say Girl, I think you want to be pregnant. So, I stop saying anything. Until one day after we found out Stacy's boyfriend was playing us. He was taking the money I gave him for rent and spent it on weed. Stacy and I were in the bathroom.

I took off my shirt when Stacy yelled, "Aisia, you have the pregnancy line."

She asked me if I saw that.

I said, "Yeah," but I thought that it was something that came with age. I didn't know.

People, please don't judge me. I was never taught anything about pregnancy. And when I asked, I was told I was delusional. So, I didn't know.

Stacy said, "We must go to the hospital."

I was worried because my birthday just passed. And even though I wouldn't say I liked the smell or taste of alcohol, I still drank. And now I could be pregnant. We went to the emergency room, which was around the corner, But Stacy didn't want to stay because it was crowded. So, we left, and she got a pregnancy test. I peed in a cup. She did the test for me, and it was positive. All I wanted to do was call my mom. I wanted her to know because that was indeed what she wanted. I got a boyfriend and I'm going to have a baby. Stacy called her family first but then I got to call my mom.

I said, "Mommy, I'm pregnant."

She asked if I was joking. She asked how I knew. I told her that I had taken a test.

She asked, "Aisia, what are you going to do?"

I told Her I was going to keep the baby. I also made an appointment at the hospital for the next day.

The next day, Jay and I went to the hospital. At the hospital, we found out that he was a boy and that I was six months pregnant. Yes, that's right, six months. I felt like lower than dirt. Six months without ever going to the doctor. Six months without prenatal anything. But once I found out, everything changed. Jay's cousin found out that she was pregnant too. She was Tawana's daughter. So, we were pregnant at the same time. We finally moved into the mix of all of that. Jay's dad came up. He had a job and took Jay with him.

Jay got paid on Fridays. Fridays were also the days we went to the doctor. So, we go and do something as a family on Fridays. A couple of times, we spent a night out. Stacy didn't like us leaving her because drama started to happen. One of Stacy's friends came to live with us. She had three kids and wanted me to write this paper stating that I would watch them while she worked. She wanted me to give her my SSN card. Now, that was going too far from me. I may not have known much about being an adult, but I knew that was a no-no. But I said oh ok, I get it for you. But I didn't and didn't plan to. One day, she got tired of it, and she and Stacy started on me. They were yelling and screaming at me. I went to my room, and I could still hear them. They were saying things like I'm a liar and all of that. Then the lady got in my face and said she would hit me. I was pregnant, so I backed out 66, and she walked out. I got my shoes on and left. I knew where I was going. I was going to Bayonne. I was going to my mom.

I walked out, and Jay followed me. He wanted me to go back and apologize like that lady just jumped in my face. Yes, Jessica Campbell came out.

"What are you talking about?"

Of course, I said, "No."

He said, "Where we are going to go."

I said, "Come with me; we're going to get to Bayonne and get our own place."

He said, "No. Go back and apologize."

"Dude, I'm the one having your son. No," and I left, and he turned around and walked home.

I waited for him to come back. Because he was my son's father, but he never came. So, I walked to Penn Station. I didn't have a dime to my name. But the thing about God is when you ask for help, he will. It started to rain while I was walking. Then I had to go to the bathroom. But I didn't stop. I wanted to show them I didn't need them. I peed on myself. I got drenched in the rain. But I kept walking, and I made it to Penn Station.

When I got there, I saw someone I knew before Jay. I asked him for some money. At first, he said he didn't have it.

I said, "OK."

He asked what he was doing there. I told him what happened. He said one second and walked away. I thought he would give me food because I knew I had to eat something. He came back with enough money to get me to Jersey City. I thanked him and told him God bless you and I got on that train. I got to Jersey City. When I got there, I was late. I got to the number 10. I asked the bus driver how much the bus was she told me. I didn't have enough. I asked this lady for a couple of dollars she gave it to me. I got on the bus. I must have smelled like pee and a wet dog. But I didn't care. I got on that bus. When I got to Bayonne, I got off the bus. I know everyone clapped, but I got there. I walked down to 18th Street. I walked into the building and walked up the stairs. I knocked on the door. My mom opened it. And I just took a breath.

My mom told me to come in and sit down. I told her I wanted to take a bath first. I took a bath, then I told her what happened. She fed me. Then I went to my room and went to sleep. Yes, she kept my room the same. No one got to sleep in my room. My mom and I went out the next day, and she said we had to get stuff for my son. She got me somethings. But we mostly did some window shopping. It was so nice to be there with my mom. Then, I called Jay to let him know that we were good. I made it to my mom's place. Then Stacy got on the phone and wanted to talk to my mom.

I don't know what they were talking about, but I heard my mom say things like she is. And yeah, I understand. I prepared myself to leave. I got back on the phone with Stacy, and she told me that Jay cut his foot. He keeps going to work, and he's hurt. She said he was walking after me when he hurt himself. So, I felt like dirt again. I got off the sofa and told my mom I had to leave. This time, she looked sad to see me go. This time, she put a smile on her face and said OK. And this time, I wasn't kicked out. We were talking about me getting my place. My mom had me go to the Housing Authority and do and application. I went and did it that day because I wanted my place. But I still left.

Chapter 12 - Being A Mother

I got back to Newark Penn Station. I returned to the same blocks I had just done a few days earlier. I got to a payphone and called my mom to say that I got to Newark ok. She said OK and told me she loved me. I told her that I loved her too. Then I called Jay. I told him I got there ok and was on my way to him. I got back. Things changed because they knew I could and would leave. And my money would go with me. I told Jay I did a housing application. He said OK, but I don't think he believed me. But the day I left to go to my mom's house, I started to have plans A, B, C, D, E, F, and g. No one was going to trap me and my son. It wasn't just me anymore; I had to think for two now.

My son was supposed to be born in June. So, it started to get hot, And I couldn't sleep. Jay and I went for a walk one night, and I told him that if he wasn't ready to be a dad, I could do it all by myself because he was three years younger than me. I was 25 at that time, and he was 22. I knew I was ready, but he was still young. He said he was ready. I said OK. And we kept on walking. I went back and forth to the hospital with Braxton Hicks contractions. Before I went in Stacy reconnected to a boyfriend she had in high school. He was well o69. She called him a Millionaire. But I didn't know. We sometimes stayed there on the weekends because he had a big house. I knew that was the house I was going to have. It was big and beautiful, and it was in a nice neighborhood. I would start writing this book, and Stacy would say things discouraging me. She would say who would read it that I was a nobody. No one would buy it. She wanted me to know I was not better than her. And I'm not. She loves d to write poems. One day, I told her she should write it and get it out there. She said no one wants to read her stuff. So, since she didn't do anything with her writing, she didn't want me to. It works for a while. I knew that's what I wanted for my son. I didn't know what I was going to do, but it was going to be big.

So, one night, I was done with this pregnancy thing, so me and Jay walked. We walked around the block two or three. After the second time, the cops were at the corner. They stopped Jay and me and asked where we were going. Jay was about to be rude. But like I told you all, I speak correctly, so I spoke. I said we lived down the block, and we were walking around the block because I was pregnant and wanted to have my baby already. One of the male cops patted me down. And they let us go. I know he was not supposed to pat me. But I didn't care because I wanted to have this baby out of me.

We went back around, and then we went inside. This time, I felt the pain in my back. I woke up at two and felt the pain. Jay asked if I wanted us to go. But we already went to the hospital two or three times. I didn't want to go, and they sentme home. Stacy said if I went too many times to the hospital, they would take my baby. I was dumb, but I would protect him with my life. I went in the bathtub because I was hot. Stacy finally was done with me yelling. She let us call 911. I called, and we went to the hospital. It went quickly. I went in. They checked me. They put me in the room, and then I pushed him out. We named him TeAmor Justin. TJ for short. I called my mom and told her I had him. I checked, and He had Ten fingers and ten toes. So, we were all good. We went home, And I had a baby. My baby. The love of my life. The only boy I loved other than my brothers.

While taking him home, something changed. I didn't care what people said about me. I didn't care if Stacy argued about not getting up in the morning. I had my baby to worry about. And if you have anxiety, having a baby makes it ten times worse. But I was going to try to be the best mom I could be a couple of weeks after his six weeks. We went to the doctor and my mom and sister Essie came to pick up TJ for a little bit. They had him for a whole week. I had to say, bring my baby back. When they brought him back, we stayed there for a little more. I guess I was getting too close to my family because Stacy said we should return to Sumter. We did, but I never told my mom to take me off the housing list. I told my mom this time that we were moving down there. We stayed in Sumter for a little then we went to Georgia. While we were still in Sumter, we stayed with Grandma Emma. Jay, TJ, and I slept on a blow-up bed in the kitchen.

One day, when I was putting TJ to sleep, Jay started arguing with me because I was not doing what he wanted. So, he wants to argue over our baby's head. He left out the door I started to cry. I rocked TJ back and forth. I told him that I loved him. I told him that he loved him too. I know because I asked him, and he said he was ready to be a dad. So, I said he loved him.

Then I thought, "What dad doesn't love his kid?" And the answer came to me, mine. Mine doesn't.

That's where Stacy's oldest brother was. His name was Wendell. We went, and I automatically connected to Wendell's wife. Her name was Duchess. I wanted to hang out with her more than be home with

Stacy; it was starting to feel like I was walking on eggshells. I was still young and naive. I was not young, but I thought Stacy cared about me and my baby. I didn't like walking on eggshells. Eventually, Stacy went to the Duchess' house because she always thought someone was talking about her because she wasn't always the easiest person to get along with. She was very condescending. Jay's brother came to live with Duchess and Wendell. I thought it would be time That TJ got to meet his uncles. And Jay gets to hang out with his brothers. But Stacy wanted to Sumter. So, we did. She said because we didn't have a car. We lived somewhere that was too far from everything. So, we moved to New Jersey. She wanted to move in with the guy she used to date in high school. So, we did. We stayed with him for a little while.

Then Stacy said that he was being mean, and she wanted to leave. So, she was going to her sister's house, and I was going home. I called my mom. I told her what happened, and she said to give her a minute. She called me back and said my cousin Winfield was there. She said he wanted to talk to me.

"I'm ok," I said

"Hey, Win," he said."Iesha, you good?"

I said, "No. I need help."

The thing about Bells. They are going to find a way to help you. So, he got his girlfriend's brother to drive him. He asked for the address, and they came to get me. When I said my cousin was coming for me, Stacy didn't believe me. Because she said they were taking too long, I said they were coming from Bayonne. Then I heard the music and my song, Iesha "by another bad creation," I knew it was my family. We got in the car. I thanked Win and the guy who was driving us. We got to my mom's house, and it was so different. My mom started to become a hoarder. She had things everywhere. But I was home. I asked Mommy if she kept up with my application forhousing. She said that I must go up there. I said OK I go in the morning. We got to hang out that night. My family got to meet TJ. And it was just cool. Like I said My family will celebrate for everything. And we celebrated Iesha coming home.

I remember walking down Broadway with Jay. He was like someone seeing for the first time. He looked all around. We worked up and down. I went to housing to find out where I was on the list. I found out they were close but not close enough. We went back to my mom's house. It was great to be with my family. It was even ok that Anthony was there because he wasn't a problem. Not because Jay could protect me. But because I did so much out in the world, I didn't care what he said. Everyone loved TJ. They want to take him everywhere. And another thing about my family is when Jay tried to argue with me, the family was like not today. Not this one. Not Iesha. He couldn't get that one o73. But it was just great being there with the family. I got to see people I didn't see for last. Like Dexter I don't even know the last seen him. I just loved it. Jay kept saying his father's side was big. I laughed because, like I said, if you count from My grandmother and grandfather, you have a nation. So yeah, big doesn't do the Bells justice.

One day, I decided to take TJ and Jay to see the two people I called my adopted parents. Margarita and Arthur. My adoptive dad didn't like Jay. He couldn't stand him, to be honest. I told him my dad doesn't like you. I said, but he doesn't like anyone. Anna and Idate. I said that to make him feel better. But I never brought anyone there. But they loved TJ. He loves the fact that he had a grandchild. I would go there and help Margarita almost every day. It was great reconnecting with them. We would still go and see Jay's side of the family. One day, his father came with his brothers to Newark. He wanted us to leave TJ with him, so we did for a couple of days until I missed my baby. Me and Jay went to go and get him. We walked in the rain back home, but I had my baby. TJ turned one at my mom's house. Win got him a Winnie the Pooh Bear stuff teddy bear. So he would know who it came from.

I also remember finally saying some of the stuff I went through. Someone in the house was arguing about money.

They would stop.

So, I got upset and yelled, "Money? Really, when I left, I didn't have a penny in my name. I had to sleep with men to have a roof over my head. I had to lie, cheat, and do things to get something to eat. You're really mad about money. You can't even begin to understand the things I went through. No one would ever understand."

And I cried because that was the first time I had said that out loud. I said what I went through, and I knew I had to. I had to say what I went through, even if it was not everything. I got something out. I needed them to know that I wasn't little Iesha. I couldn't be. I've seen too much. I have been through too much. After that, Mommy just held me, but she didn't know. The little girl who left her house wasn't the girl who returned, not only because she was a mommy.

Chapter 13 - What Do I Do Now

One day, TJ had been sick for two days straight. I had planned to take him to the doctor on Monday, but it was only Saturday. As I tried to feed him his medicine, he woke up, and we went into my mom's room to watch TV. Essie, my sister, was with us. I noticed TJ wasn't eating, and when I mentioned it, Essie took him from me, saying he was wet. I asked her to bring me a diaper from the living room. She got up and left the room, and I laid TJ down on the bed. Then it happened. He was staring straight at the ceiling, and I knew what was going on. Panicked, I yelled for Essie to call 911 because TJ was having a seizure. I remember my mom telling me stories from when I was little, saying I would stare at the wall during seizures. As soon as I yelled, TJ started to shake violently. I called 911 and explained the situation. The ambulance arrived quickly, but I knew I needed someone else there. I told Essie to go get Mommy, who was at the laundromat, and Jay, who was at work. Despite needing someone, I focused on comforting my baby, who needed me the most. We rushed to the hospital in the ambulance, hoping for the best.

TJ remained unconscious as we rushed to the hospital, and he suffered another seizure in the ambulance. When we arrived, I called Jay to inform him, but he misunderstood, thinking I had just mentioned TJ wasn't feeling well. I didn't realize this misunderstanding until later. Feeling frustrated and panicked, I asked Jay to come to the hospital, but he explained he was out of town and couldn't make it. I couldn't comprehend why he couldn't drop everything for his son, but all I managed to say was "Okay, bye" before hanging up.

Entering TJ's room, I witnessed him having another seizure, and the doctors promptly ushered me out. I understood they were doing their best to help him, but I desperately wanted to be by my baby's side.

My mom rushed in, and I ran into her arms, repeating over and over, "He's not waking up. He won't wake up. That's not good."

My mom asked me some questions, trying to calm me down, and I told her about TJ being with the doctors, but they wouldn't let me in.

Suddenly, TJ seemed to stir, crying for me, but then slipped into another seizure. The doctors conferred silently, and I realized they were planning to take him for an X-ray. Nodding my agreement, my mom and I accompanied them to the waiting room, where I marveled at how my mom managed this at just 19. She admitted it wasn't easy but assured me she did what she had to. I silently acknowledged her strength.

The wait for the X-ray felt endless, but eventually, they returned with the results. The doctors informed us they needed to transfer TJ to another hospital. I asked my mom to stay until we left, and she agreed. As I realized Jay needed to get home, I prepared to make the difficult call.

Feeling a mix of disappointment and anger, I waited a little longer at the hospital, hoping Jay would show up, but he never did. Eventually, I called my mom's house, hoping against hope that Jay wasn't there, that he had just been running late. However, Win answered the phone, confirming my fears that Jay was indeed at my mom's house. I asked for Jay, trying to keep my frustration in check, but he was there.

When I questioned why he hadn't come to the hospital, he simply said he was tired and thought it was me, not TJ, who needed help. Despite my boiling emotions, I bit back the words I wanted to say.

Instead, I tersely replied, "Okay," knowing I couldn't afford a confrontation while in the midst of a crisis.

I briefed him on TJ's condition and what had happened, and all he could muster was a feeble "wow."

The doctor eventually deemed TJ stable enough for transfer, and when the ambulance arrived, I instructed my mom to relay a message to Jay: that he was an idiot. With a tight hug from my mom, I carried TJ into the ambulance bound for the other hospital, trying to push aside the anger and focus on getting my son the care he needed.

Upon arriving at the other hospital, one of the EMTs kindly handed me some money to grab food for myself. It was a thoughtful gesture, but in the whirlwind of emotions, I couldn't focus on my own needs. I thought, "I don't need to eat. I need my son to wake up. I need him home with me, healthy and lively." Still, I managed a grateful "thank you" and "God bless you" before we headed to TJ's room.

Feeling overwhelmed, I decided to call Jay, knowing he needed to be updated as TJ's father. It also served as a brief distraction from the fear and worry gripping me. I informed him that we had arrived at the hospital. Desperately seeking some semblance of normalcy, I asked what he was up to.

His response hit me like a blow: He was drinking and hanging out with my cousin. Anger surged within me at his casualness and apparent indifference to the gravity of the situation. But I pushed it aside, focusing instead on the task at hand: ensuring TJ received the care he needed.

Fueled by frustration and exhaustion, I confronted Jay with the anger that had been simmering beneath the surface.

"You said you'd try to come to the hospital to see your son, but you're drinking. Oh, that's right, I had him by myself," I yelled, my words dripping with resentment.

His feeble excuse of having a long day and needing to unwind only fueled my anger further. With a terse "Okay, Jay, bye," I ended the call, seething with frustration.

Sinking into a chair, I muttered to myself about his idiocy, shaking my head in disbelief. Desperate for some sense of normalcy, I turned on cartoons on the TV, hoping TJ might find comfort in the familiar sounds. I couldn't be sure if it worked, but it helped ease my own tension, if only slightly.

Realizing I hadn't taken care of myself in hours, I stole a quick shower, afraid to be away from TJ for too long. I grabbed a bite to eat from the kitchen, along with some water, before returning to his room. I tried to rest, but the worry gnawed at me all night long. I prayed fervently, begging for TJ's recovery.

Morning finally brought the relief I had been praying for. My son woke up. The flood of emotions was indescribable, a mix of overwhelming joy and immense gratitude. He drifted in and out of sleep, but seeing him awake filled me with hope. We stayed at the hospital for three days until TJ was stable enough to go home.

Returning to my mom's house, all I wanted to do was lash out at Jay. But instead, I focused on my baby, watching over him like a hawk, cherishing every moment we had together.

One day, TJ wasn't feeling well again, and this time, I was determined to take action. I decided to take him to the hospital. However, things took an unexpected turn when the nurse asked us to stay for a long time. I couldn't understand why until they mentioned that my mom and I smelled like cat pee, prompting them to call D.Y.S.F. on me.

The situation escalated quickly, and D.Y.S.F took us back to the house, only to find it unprepared for anyone to stay. Consequently, they insisted that we all leave. Win went with his girlfriend to her parents' house while my mom, the kids, Jay, TJ, and I ended up in a hotel for the night. The following day, I awaited the case worker's arrival, getting TJ dressed and ready.

When the case worker came, she asked if we had somewhere to go. Although my mom and the kids went back home, they only wanted TJ and me to find a place to stay. So, I suggested Margarita's house. The caseworker accompanied us there and explained the situation to Margarita, who agreed to let us stay.

However, there was a complication as my dad stated that TJ and I could stay, but not Jay, asserting that he wasn't a dad. Faced with this dilemma, I urged Jay to see if he could stay with my cousin Velda, which he agreed to.

Feeling overwhelmed and inadequate, I prayed fervently for a sign that everything would turn out okay. Just then, a song called "Redeemed" by Big Daddy Weave started playing on the radio. Its lyrics resonated deeply with me, offering words of hope and redemption in the midst of struggles and failures. I found solace in the song, listening to it repeatedly and shedding tears of relief.

Eventually, Margarita persuaded my dad to allow Jay to stay, albeit reluctantly. Meanwhile, my mom worked tirelessly to clean and prepare the house for our return. Eventually, we went back home, and D.Y.F.S closed the case, marking the end of a challenging ordeal.

One day, Stacy called me, informing me that Jay's brothers needed us to pick them up. However, it turned out that only one of them needed assistance, as the other two had alternative arrangements. I couldn't accept leaving one brother behind, so I immediately decided that we had to go to Sumter.

With Jay, TJ, and me, we headed out to help his brother. Mentally preparing myself for the task ahead, I focused on the goal of bringing his brother back with us. Upon arrival, I switched into business mode, determined to handle the situation efficiently. I inquired about the whereabouts of the kids and who we needed to speak with, considering my income and Jay's familial connection might facilitate a solution where we could assist them all.

I even had an application ready for housing, confident that I could secure a place for all of us. I was in full-on planning mode, ready to take charge of the situation. However, my plans came crashing down when I discovered that it was all a lie, perhaps just to persuade us to live with Stacy.

Refusing to be trapped in the same situation again, I decided to leave the house. We went to visit Jay's brothers and ended up staying with Stacy temporarily, but this time, I was determined not to be taken advantage of.

On my birthday, Stacy prepared a lovely dinner and brought along a cake and some alcohol. Despite her efforts, something inside me urged me not to drink it, although it wasn't due to disliking the taste or smell. Stacy questioned why I wasn't drinking on my birthday. The next day, a feeling of unease lingered, prompting me to suggest to Jay that we go to the hospital for a pregnancy test. Walking towards the hospital, we stumbled upon a Christian center offering free pregnancy tests. We decided to take advantage of it, and the test came back positive. I had sensed it all along.

I called my mom to share the news and learned that my little sister Mary was also pregnant. Mom revealed they were uncertain about the father, but I suspected her new boyfriend. Though Mom didn't confront him directly, I couldn't shake the feeling that he was lying. Feeling furious, I insisted on going to the doctor's but didn't want to return home afterward. Jay suggested visiting his mom at the park, where TJ could meet his grandmother. It felt right for TJ to know both sides of his family.

When we arrived, Grandma was thrilled to see TJ and captured precious moments with photos. It warmed my heart to see TJ surrounded by family. Mary eventually gave birth to a baby girl named Tina. One day, while Tina was home with them, I called and noticed she was quiet. When I inquired, Mom mentioned she was asleep. Later, when I asked for Essie, Mom whispered to her about my suspicion, though I chose not to dwell on it. Instead, I invited Essie to visit me, covering her expenses for the trip, eager to spend time with her family.

Now that Essie was with me, I felt like I had a real family. I cherished her presence, and we grew closer each day. Finding out that I was expecting a girl, we decided to name her Shanta after our grandma. Essie's arrival brought joy, and I greeted her with a warm hug, thrilled to have her by my side. She shared her excitement about seeing me, too, and we spent quality time together, enjoying each other's company.

Now, with Essie by my side, I truly felt like I had a family. The news of expecting a baby girl and naming her Shanta after our grandma filled me with joy. Essie's arrival brought even more happiness despite Stacy's attempts to stir up drama. Initially, Stacy seemed cordial, but her true colors soon surfaced.

Essie and I spent quality time together, attending my doctor's appointments and relishing each other's company. She shared details about our family back home, including a troubling incident involving Tina's father. It saddened me to hear about the chaos and the involvement of authorities, but I promised Essie I would come back soon to help.

Meanwhile, Jay's parents went through a breakup, and his father found a new girlfriend who rubbed me the wrong way. She seemed disdainful towards us and had little patience for children, spending her time drinking excessively. Despite the challenges, Essie and Jay took turns accompanying me to doctor's appointments.

Living near train tracks posed its own dangers, as one day, while crossing them with Jay, I felt a sudden sensation of the baby dropping. It was a startling moment, but it reinforced the reality of impending motherhood.

A few days later, I woke up with intense pain in my legs, signaling that labor had begun. I turned to Jay and informed him that it was time. He hurried to get Stacy's help, closing the door behind him. Essie, who had been sleeping on the sofa, also woke up and assisted me to the sofa. She was irritated with Jay for closing the door, but there was no time to dwell on it.

Stacy questioned why I always went into labor when everyone was asleep, but I reassured her it wasn't intentional. They called for an ambulance, but the response was delayed due to a passing train. Eventually, the ambulance arrived, and as they strapped me onto the gurney, I knew the baby was coming. I informed the EMTs, who advised me to try to hold her in, which seemed impossible.

Upon reaching the hospital, I reiterated to the medical staff about my history of fast labor, but it seemed they either didn't believe me or had forgotten. When I felt the urge to push, they told me to resist, which was challenging. Jay was directed to the waiting room while I changed into hospital attire, a difficult task in my condition. Fortunately, the doctor arrived promptly, and upon assessing the situation, she urgently called for Jay.

Moments later, with Jay by my side, looking pale, I held my baby girl in my arms, feeling a rush of overwhelming joy and relief. Despite the chaotic circumstances, the sight of our newborn daughter filled us with profound happiness.

As I mentioned, we named her Shanta Rosa. She had the cutest mean mug, and whenever Jay held her, I could see the smile on his face from a mile away. When we first arrived, Jay went to catch some sleep, leaving just Shanta and me. Thankfully, she was a good baby; she only cried when she needed her diaper changed. Surprisingly, she slept through the night right from the start, which made things easier.

The rest of the day was quite unusual. Stacy showed up first, which was unexpected because she hadn't visited me in the hospital. Then the kids' grandmother arrived, which was a pleasant surprise since it brought some family comfort. Later, I realized Stacy's motive for coming was probably to show off. However, Essie came to stay the night with me, which I appreciated.

The day I left the hospital with my baby girl happened to be on Halloween. Jay's dad and his new girlfriend were there. She used to claim that my son had taken something from her bag, so her presence made me uneasy. Inside, Jay's dad and his girlfriend had prepared a cake for Shanta Rosa. Stacy made a comment insinuating that she might as well be considered the kids' grandma. I promptly corrected her, stating that they have two grandmas, thank you very much.

Upon leaving the hospital, I decided to take TJ trick-or-treating, despite knowing it might not have been the best idea. But with two babies in tow, we ventured out for some Halloween fun, accompanied by Essie, Stacy, and Ella.

Chapter 14 - My Own Place

It was an amazing experience to have both my little girl and my little boy. Essie extended her stay a bit longer because I wanted her to accompany me to Georgia for Thanksgiving at Duchess and Wendell's house. We had a blast there, especially enjoying a drink called Blue one and done, which had a sneaky kick despite its innocuous taste. Seeing Essie, who was over 21, indulge alongside me reminded me of how quickly time flies—she was still my little girl in my eyes, even though she was all grown up. But being there for her, taking care of her, brought me immense joy. Our stay was filled with laughter, like the time TJ barged into Duchess's room with his signature morning enthusiasm, only to be playfully reprimanded.

Upon returning home, Essie fell ill, prompting me to send her back home the following month. I wished I could have accompanied her. After Essie's departure, Stacy resumed her usual antics. Not long after, Jay and I also left, returning to my mom's house. This time, housing discovered Jay's presence, prompting me to encourage him to stay at the shelter so we could secure our own place. And we did! Getting my own apartment was a momentous occasion—I couldn't contain my excitement.

Despite my mom never removing me from her lease, she generously supported me, even though it meant her rent might have been reduced. Reconnecting with Anna and Diana during my time at my mom's house was a blessing. I shared with them the trials and tribulations I endured while living with Stacy. Diana, in particular, empathized with me, having gone through similar experiences.

Our bond deepened as we spent every day together, chatting on the phone incessantly. Getting my first cellphone, even if it wasn't touchscreen, felt like a milestone. It was mine, bought with my own money. Being a mother of two with my friends by my side filled me with happiness. We dubbed ourselves sisters, akin to the female versions of the Three Musketeers.

Amidst all this, I received a surprising call from Stacy, who asked if Essie had gained weight. Perplexed, I asked Essie to show me her stomach, but our sister Blabbermouth Mary tagged along. Despite Essie's silent plea for silence, I subtly suggested she could consider fixing her outie bellybutton, which she seemed grateful for. Urging her to inform Mom about her pregnancy and ensuring she sought medical attention, I hoped she would follow through despite her reluctance to confide in Mom.

Then came the day when Essie went to get her hair done, and the next morning, as I prepared breakfast, I entered her room to inquire about her appetite. But with one glance at her, I knew she was in labor. I immediately asked if she needed to go to the hospital, to which she responded affirmatively.

Waking my brother and discovering Mom was at the laundromat, I instructed him to fetch her while I calmly informed Mom about Essie's situation. It was the first time Mom had heard about Essie's pregnancy, and as Essie tearfully confirmed the news, I couldn't help but feel relieved that Mom's reaction was not one of anger or accusation.

Accompanying Essie to the hospital, I was surprised by the nurses' initial lack of urgency in assessing her condition. However, after finally taking her upstairs and conducting an examination, they determined she was three centimeters dilated. Essie was incredulous, having endured labor pains all night long. Though she desired pain medication, they refused, citing her advanced labor stage. Despite her discomfort, I reassured her that relief would come once the baby was born.

They said Essie was too far along for pain medication. Essie insisted they were lying, convinced they just didn't want to give it to her. She refused to entertain their explanations.

Finally, my mom arrived, bringing lunch for me, the first meal I'd had all day. I devoured it eagerly, then walked back into the room to find that Essie's baby had been born. They named her Imani, and I was thrilled to be an auntie once again. It was great because all our children were around the same age, so Essie and I often took them to the park and did a lot together with our babies.

In June of that year, I secured our own place. It felt like a significant step toward adulthood. My mom helped me move in, and we have a tradition of saying "I'm dancing with you" instead of "I'm proud of you," signifying our immense pride in each other. TJ had his own room, and I made sure to set it up with all his favorite things. Shanta and I shared a room, and I made sure to get cable so the kids could enjoy watching cartoons.

Jay initially would go back to the shelter because they promised him an apartment there, and his job would pick him up from the shelter. But one day, he decided he'd had enough of going back and forth and chose to stay.

One day, my mom's aunt Rachel passed away, and we went to her house in Hoboken. It was where my grandfather had passed away, and going through her belongings was a nostalgic journey. I stumbled upon pictures of my mom from before I was born and got to reconnect with family I hadn't seen in a long time. Seeing my cousin Christina there, confidently being herself, was eye-opening. It made me question why I was hiding in the closet. I've known who I am since I was 8, and my mom has known me since I was 15, so why was I still hiding? While I love being a mom, I realized I hated not being true to myself. My cousin's fearless attitude inspired me to embrace my true self.

Chapter 15 - Margarita, I Do Love You

I would often visit Margarita at her house to help her with tasks since she and her husband were older. One day, while we were in the backyard, she asked why I had left her. I explained that the hospital had called her, but she refused to take me back. Seeing her cry, I felt terrible, and it reminded me of the time I expressed my feelings to my mom about feeling abandoned. It was a harsh truth, but not everyone can handle it. I apologized, recognizing the hurt my words caused. Leaving that day, I reflected on my actions, realizing I had deeply wounded her with my words. There were times when I wished my words could cut through, like when I lived with Stacy, to express my true feelings. But back then, I didn't want to hurt her, knowing she had taken me in when no one else would. So, I returned, apologized again, and hugged her.

Soon, Anna returned from Texas, and I got to see both Margarita and Anna at the same time. Anna took me to New York for my birthday, wanting to take pictures for her portfolio. While I'm quite awkward when it comes to being photographed, I obliged for her. She found it amusing when I mentioned I don't usually go to New York. After our trip, Diana wanted to do something together. She and her husband were living with her dad, similar to how we all lived with our parents initially. Eventually, I got my own place, followed by Diana and her husband getting theirs, conveniently just a few blocks away from mine.

When Diana visited my new place, I felt a sense of adulthood. She got to meet Jay and my babies. Since Diana's husband worked nights, I offered to spend the first night with her. We enjoyed watching music videos and had a great time together. Diana always had a funny habit of glancing at me whenever there was an attractive girl singing on TV, which never failed to make me laugh. Diana and I often discussed how we looked forward to the day when my son would attend the same school we did. I felt a strong connection with Diana, and I could envision a future with her. I recall picking Diana up from work on occasion, waiting for her to finish her shift, and then heading back to her house.

One day, while we were outside a grocery store, I asked Diana if she enjoyed sex with men. She mentioned she enjoyed it with her husband. This made me question if perhaps my lack of enjoyment stemmed from myself rather than my partners. Diana, being the quiet introvert she was, made me wonder if it was just me. Although both Anna and Diana were my friends, I felt closer to Diana. I longed to find someone like her. I often attended Diana's church with her, although I couldn't stay all day due to my responsibilities with my children. I admired Diana's involvement in the church choir and praise dancing. I never explicitly told Diana how I felt, but I always suspected she knew. She remains the one that got away, my "what if." Arthur's sister and niece came to New Jersey due to his sister's illness, staying with Arthur and Margarita, much to Margarita's displeasure.

One day, I went to Margarita's house to help her with something. After we finished our task, she asked me to fetch her a can of

Strawberry, a strawberry margarita in a can. Despite knowing I shouldn't have, I complied. But then she asked for two more, and I reluctantly got them as well. She drank those down quickly and then requested two more. Realizing it was getting out of hand, I made an excuse to leave, knowing that if I wasn't there, she couldn't keep asking for more. I went to pick up Diana, and we headed home. However, Diana called me soon after, saying that Anna needed us urgently as she had been kicked out. I called Anna and told her to come to my house, then waited as long as I could. However, I eventually fell asleep, only to wake up in the morning and realize Anna hadn't shown up. When I called Diana, she informed me that Anna had indeed come to her house. Rushing over to Diana's, I found it crowded. I ended up taking Anna and Arthur's sister and niece back to my place. I learned that Arthur's sister had cancer and was going to a hospital for treatment, but they had clashed with Margarita, resulting in Anna being hit by Margarita. Consequently, Anna left along with Arthur's sister and niece. Back at my place, Arthur's sister went to the hospital, while Anna and the niece stayed with me. Anna's boyfriend would often come over, and we'd hang out and have fun. However, the niece's behavior became problematic as she started staying out all night, using her mother's illness as an excuse to party. Eventually, she left Bayonne. Anna then made plans for another girl from our high school to come up to New Jersey to live with her and her boyfriend.

I still continued to pick up Diana despite Anna's apparent dislike for it. She'd make comments about why I was leaving her to go get Diana, insisting that Margarita was more like our mom, so we were sisters. However, I didn't let Anna's remarks deter me; I would always go and pick up Diana. There was just something different about Diana that compelled me to do so. On Diana's birthday, I'd get her balloons, even though we both feared them. She'd joke that I thought I was funny. Diana often shared anecdotes about a girl from our church, mentioning that she thought the girl might be gay because she always hugged her. I found it amusing because I never got that impression.

One day, Anna's boyfriend took us to pick up Heather, a girl who attended our school. From the moment I met Heather, I liked her. For me, it's either an immediate like or dislike when I meet someone, and with Heather, it was definitely the former. I was so obvious about it, being a Bell, you'd know when I was fluttering. During our time together, we played "Never Have I Ever," and I discovered Heather was attracted to black people. However, I later realized it was specifically black girls, not guys. Despite our differences, we found common ground, especially in our love for reading. Heather mentioned she usually keeps to herself but found it easy to talk to me. One night, as we sat on my kitchen floor, we talked for hours. Jay, sensing my feelings for Heather, remarked that he could tell. I would agree, saying, "I know, she's great, right?" But when Heather expressed her concerns about my having kids and her desire to remain child-free, I reassured her that my babies come first. When Heather told me to stop fluttering, I complied, perhaps surprising her with how quickly I did. It seemed like she didn't expect me to give up so easily because she came after me. I couldn't help but feel a sense of irony, considering I had pursued her for so long, and now she seemed interested in me. But I decided that if she wanted me, she'd have to chase me; I wasn't going to make it easy. Eventually, unable to keep my feelings to myself, I confided in Diana about what was happening with Heather, even though I knew I probably shouldn't have, judging from her reaction. But I needed to share it with someone.

One day, Anna and I went to Margarita's house to collect some of her belongings. I greeted Margarita with a hug when we arrived, and Anna did the same before heading inside to gather her things. As I stayed outside, Margarita remarked, "You don't love me anymore." I assured her that I did, explaining that I had been busy lately. Despite my reassurances, I could sense a disconnect. Shortly after, Anna, Heather, and Anna's boyfriend moved into a new place together. While I was okay with their decision, I wasn't prepared for how Anna's behavior towards me would change. It felt like she suddenly considered me insignificant, going silent on me. I confided in Jay and Diana, desperate to understand what I might have done wrong. The uncertainty and feeling of rejection left me in tears many nights.

Then, one day, I received a missed call from Anna, who had a voicemail asking me to call her back. My heart leaped with joy, thinking she might want to reconcile. When I returned her call, Anna delivered two words that shattered my world: "Mommy died." I dropped the phone in shock, hearing her call out my name. After picking it up, she explained that Dad found Mom on the floor at home, unresponsive. Despite calling for help, she was pronounced dead at the hospital. All I could think was, "I thought I had more time." I regretted the moments of anger and distance between us, believing there would always be a chance to reconcile. When Anna couldn't reach Dad, I felt even more helpless. After saying our goodbyes, my face must have betrayed my turmoil, as Jay noticed and asked if I was okay. Through tears, I revealed that my mom had passed away. When Jay asked which mom, I clarified it was Margarita. Concerned about Dad, I admitted I didn't know how he was doing, as he wasn't answering the phone. Jay offered to accompany me, and I agreed, feeling a desperate need for my own mother's presence. Taking the kids, we went to Margarita's house to bring her with us. Arriving at Dad's house, he was in the living room, but I couldn't bring myself to sit down. I was overwhelmed with grief, unsure how to navigate this new reality without my mom.

While at the wake with Diana, someone approached me and offered condolences for my loss. Their gesture caught me off guard because, technically, I wasn't her biological daughter, and my kids weren't her biological grandchildren. But they understood that she was my mom, and I was her daughter, and my kids were her grandkids. To that person, I'm grateful for their kindness. After that day, I never returned to Margarita's house. Anna also drifted out of my life, but it was okay because I still had Diana. Margarita always believed in me, often expressing her conviction that I would write a book and achieve success. She encouraged me not to forget her and Dad. I assured her that I would never forget them. She even asked me to be her ghostwriter and pen her story, but unfortunately, I never had the opportunity to do so. Margarita urged me to use my experiences to help others, to let them know that things get better. She wanted me to assist people like us who faced struggles and challenges. I hope she's watching from above and feeling proud of me. I'm following her wishes, Margarita, and I love you.

Chapter 16 – My Little Surprise

One day, I had the same feeling. I felt like I was pregnant again. I just found out Essie was going to have a baby boy. But I took a test, and yes, I was pregnant. I found out on Monday and Friday I was bleeding. I checked online, and it said it was fine. But I went to the doctor anyway.

When I got there, I told the doctor's what happened. I told them that I took a pregnancy test, and it said that I was pregnant, but then I started to bleed. The doctor gave me a pregnancy test through blood and then an ultrasound.

Again, the test said I was pregnant, but the ultrasound showed the was no baby. They sent me to the Emergency Room, and then I found out I lost my baby. I told Jay, and all he said was I thought you said it was ok to bleed and the beginning stages.

I hung up because that's not what I wanted to hear. My uncle's girlfriend, "My aunt Tosha," called me. I forgot why because I was in a daze. She asked what I was doing. I told her that I just left the hospital. She asked me why I was there. I told her I just lost the baby that I just told her I was pregnant with. She asked if I was walking. I told her yes, I was. She said to stay where I was and that my cousin would come and get me.

So, I waited there, and my cousin came to get me. She dropped me off at my house. I went straight to bed. The next day, I just held my kids. I didn't talk to anyone. I just held my kids. Jay didn't understand what happened. Neither did I. I had to say I had three pregnancies and two living babies. How does that sound? I didn't want to talk about it. I would say anything; I just moved passed it because it was too hard. I just stopped talking about it. I didn't even know fit my baby was going to be a boy or a girl. Then Jay left to go back to Sumter. Because Housing found out he was living with me, and he didn't want to live in a shelter again. So, he left.

Before he left thought we slept together. And I was pregnant again. This time, I didn't say anything in the beginning. I found out Essie was having a baby boy. She went into labor early, and she had her first son. She named him Maddy. So, we were kind of tired. She had one girl and one boy. I had one boy and one girl. I got a little taste of had it felt to be a single mom. And I knew I could do it. Housing found out Jay was living with me again.

Before Jay left, it was the beginning of March my mom wanted to take me out for my birthday. We went to my mom's favorite Chinese restaurant. It was called Eat Rice. So we ate there, and then we went to D and D's. I went in with my mom.

As I went in, I saw this lady at the front door. I told my mom that I was going to go outside so she could hurry up. When I went outside, I saw the same lady. She had a lot of stuff, so I asked her if she needed help. She looked at me surprised because she expected me to ask her that. She said that's why she shouldn't judge a book by its cover.

I laughed but didn't really get it. We started to talk. She did something all lesbians do when we want to know if the person we are talking to is gay or at least ok with it. She brought up her girlfriend nonchalantly. We talked some more. I found out she was a Pieces, too. But she was born in February. If you don't understand why that's important, then you're not a Piece. Anyway, she found out that I liked women too. She gave me her number. I told her I had a compact relationship. We talked for a while; then, I had to leave and go home.

Going home to my babies was great, but going home to a man was not. Jay and I became more of a roommate than boyfriend and girlfriend. I didn't see myself as his girlfriend. But we were. The lady's name was America, but she went by Poca. We hung out a couple of times.

The first time, she went to the gym, and then she went to a tanning place. She walked me crossed the street to take the bus home. My mom called me while I was with her, and she asked if I had any money because she had to go to court for Tina. I told her that I didn't have any money.

My mom said OK. When I hung up the phone, Poca asked what happened. I told her that my mom needed money for something, but I didn't have it.

Poca gave me 280 dollars. I said thank you. I waited until she got on the bus and walked down the street. We were already on 18th Street. I waited because of two reasons I didn't want to just leave her, and I didn't want Poca to know where I came from.

Don't get me wrong, I was proud of where I came from. I just didn't think she understood where I came from. She would talk about being a Sprint runner in the Olympics. She would say she has all this money. So, I didn't think that she would understand me. And no, I didn't think she was better than me, but I thought she would talk about it.

I gave my mom the money she needed, and then I went home. Soon after Jay left, the kids and I left. We went to Sumter on the train. Before I left, I asked Dannie if she had a suitcase so I could pack some of the kids' stuff. She gave it to me I told her I would send it back to her, but I never got the chance to. She also asked why I was going down there. She basically bragged me to stay.

I told her I wasn't going to live with Starr I was going to live with Jay's mom. I told her that we talked on the phone and we were getting close. Diana said OK, but I knew she didn't want me to leave. I really didn't want to go too.

Chapter 17 – A Whirlwind

The kids and I got to Sumter and we were with their family. It was great because my kids got to know their grandma. They got to see their uncles. I loved them getting to know their family because that was something I promised myself when I was a little girl. I told myself three things: I said I would have my babies by the same man, my kids would know their father, and they would know their family. I never wanted my kids to feel alone. I never wanted them to feel like they didn't belong anywhere. I wanted them to know where they came from.

So, living there was something I needed for my family. I told the kid's grandma that I liked girls. I believe she wondered why I was with her son. I knew she knew that I was good to him in the fact that I made sure he had what he needed, but we both knew I wasn't good for the fact that I didn't even like men. I know, I know, I should have never been with him.

I should have just let him find someone better for him. But at night, Jay would tell me how everyone in his life let him down. In hindsight, I was letting him down by staying with him. I didn't want to be another letdown.

I was worse when we lived with Stacy because she would say things like, "Don't you want to be like the family on the TV." Or "Look at the shows you like so much that could be you two."

I would look at my kids, and I didn't want them to not have their dad like I didn't. So, I stayed. While I was, Shanta and I got closer.

She loved seeing her grandkids. We got so close I called her mom. I just didn't like the way her boyfriend treated her. He reminded me of Anthony. Shanna reminded me of my mom. So, I wanted to protect him because I was not a child anymore. Now listen, don't get me wrong, I am not a fighter, but I'm not going to back down either.

So, one day, her boyfriend made her cry again I was done with that. So, instead of punching him because I was pregnant and I didn't want him to push me and hurt my baby. I didn't know what he was going to do. He was drunk and high, so I didn't know how he would handle me hitting him. So, I punch a door.

The only thing was the door was metal. It didn't hurt as bad as I thought a broken bone would feel like. Shanta told Jay to take me to the hospital. So, he did. I went into the ER, and as soon as the doctor touched me, I felt it. I felt the pain.

They told me I broke it in two different places. Great, I was a mom of two and pregnant with my third one. And I did something stupid. I went through the six weeks with the break, and it was ok. Shanta was great. She made sure I had everything I wanted when I was pregnant. Shanta and I would go to a meeting every day.

At first, I would just go with her, but then I went for me too. It was to help people who had a drug addiction. Soon, we decided that the one bedroom we lived in was too small for all of us. And it was closer to the meetings. So, we moved there because it was bigger, and it was better for our baby to come home.

I got someone to be my sponsor. She said sure, but I need you to call me every day for 30 days. I was like, what? I didn't like the phone.

I didn't like talking on the phone. But I did it. While I was done there, I didn't forget my family back home.

One day, I called back home, and my mom said she got kicked out of housing. I called my sponsor, upset. She said, "Aisia breathe. Your feeling is valid." Those four words were everything to me. I was always told that I felt too deeply.

But someone validating my feelings was great. She went on to say, "You're down here. What are you going to do for your siblings down here?"

She said, "Your mom is their mom, so she is going to take care of them." I thought, but I'm their sister I need to help them. I wasn't there for Tina, and she got taken. I didn't want my siblings taken. I was talking about Essie or Anthony because they were adults. But even though Mary and Patrick are technically adults, too, they have autism.

They couldn't take care of themselves. But she didn't know that, so I kind of let it go. Whenever I called home, my mom would be asked when I was coming home. I would tell her that I was coming home soon. I knew that was true. Not that I didn't like living where I was. I just knew that I was going to get myself out of being Jay's girlfriend.

I found out I was having a baby boy. I told the doctor that I was going to have my tubes tied. They said they don't tie tubes. They said they burn them. I said OK, that is fine. They looked at me confused because I was 29 and I only had three babies. I told them no; I was 29 and already had three living babies.

They asked a couple of times if I was sure. I said yes. I went to a doctor's appointment when I started to ask a bunch of questions. This was a very hard pregnancy. I was always sick, not just in the first trimester. I was ready to have this baby. Jay and I went home, and I knew I was going to have him soon. I got my bag ready. And since he was my last baby, I savored every moment. I pack his stuff repeatedly. I wasn't told I was going to have another baby. I was happy my family was complete.

One night, again at night I started to have pain. The funny thing was I was so close to my due date. I was a week away with the other two I was two weeks. I was sure when I conceived him because of the miscarriage I had right before I conceived him. I went in that night, and the next morning, I was fine. But the doctor said that they weren't going to send me home. Because they remembered that I had quit labor, and they didn't want me to have him at home.

So, they said that they were going to induce my labor. I thought that was fine because I had two babies before without any meds. So, I would be fine. I thought I was a G I got this. But the medicine they gave me was unworldly. They put an I.V. in my arm and gave me medicines through that. Then, the epidural doctor came in and told me everything they said before. I told her I didn't need it. I had two babies naturally; I don't need it.

They said OK and left. Then it hit me. Like I said, I had quit labor, so even the medicine they gave me would be faster. I told Jay to run and get that doctor back. He must have seen that I was serious because he knew I was big on natural birth.

So, he ran. The other doctor came in, too. The doctor gave me the epidural. But it was too late because my baby was on his way. I went through so much pain that I felt like I was going to pass out.

Jay must have seen this because he went pale. The baby came out, and I was done. I could stay alert. I looked at Jay. He was sitting down now because he thought I was going to die. Then I looked down, and I thought to myself, your baby is going to fall. I felt like out was out of my body. I yell at myself get your baby. So, I got done, it felt like I did this over my head, but I grabbed my baby, and I was fine. I came back. He brought me back to reality.

I heard Jay finally breathe. The doctor said she wanted to weigh my baby because he was small. He also had a little jaundice, so he had to stay under the lights in the nursery. And he failed his hearing test on his right side. But he was here. I planned on breastfeeding him, so I had to go to the nursery to feed him.

The next day, he was allowed to be with me. We named him Johnny Mitch. So, there it was. I was a mom of three babies under school age. Johnny was a momma's boy from every start. He didn't want anyone, not his dad, not his uncle; he just wanted me. But the only time I got a break was when his grandma got him. He was fine with her because she was a woman. Who he loved to be with. He would have to go with me to the meetings. I had to take him everywhere because if I didn't, he would scream his lungs out.

Even when I started to pump the milk, he didn't want to stay with anyone. If I did leave him, you would hear him screaming down the block. I would go inside, and as soon as I walked in, he would stop. I felt like he smelled me. Shanta was my big helper. She loved to help with the new baby even though she was only two. I got my tubes burned a couple of days later. It was one step of me walking away from Jay. I needed to gain control of my life.

Chapter 18 – How Did I Get Here

Soon, something bad happened, and we got kicked out. I had a phone, so I called my sponsor, and she said she would get the kids and myself a room but not Shanta and hers. I didn't know how to tell her, so I told her son what was told to me. I didn't know, but he told her. So, we went to the hotel for a night. Then she took me and the kids to another one of her spondees. I got to get close to her. We had a lot in common. Shanta didn't like her family being with this lady. They didn't get along.

One day, the group was going on a trip she paid for me to go, but she said she didn't want to go. The kids stayed with Shanna and their dad. I had a great time.

Another lady who went to the same meetings thought that the kids shouldn't live with her. So, she called Tawana. Tawana called Stacy, and Stacy called me. She told me to leave. I told her the lady was being nice to us. She took us in when she didn't have to.

Stacy was on speaker, and she asked who said something and told me not to say anything. But it was too late. The lady heard. She got mad and called her. Stacy got mad at me, But I said that she was on the speaker. She said oh and hung up.

We lived with the lady for a while until one day. She said she was going to do something. I got to meet her sister, and when she didn't come home, I called her. I went to bed with the kids, but she wasn't back yet. I went to the meeting, and I told my sponsor. Her sponsor heard me and said I should go because her sister probably wanted me out. I said OK. Me and the kids left, and we followed Jay to Stacy's house again. Yes, we were back at Stacy's house. I felt terrible. It was a lot in a very short amount of time. I went into the hospital for the first time in years. But when I came out, I knew what I was going to do.

I told Jay finally that I was a lesbian, and I wasn't going to be with him anymore as boyfriend and girlfriend. I told him that we could work together to parent our kids, but there was nothing else between us. He said OK. But he changed towards me. But I didn't care. I got to be myself, finally. I got TJ into school.

The school was hard for him. I taught him how to spell his name by making up a song. He got it after that. The teacher would complain about him. But I thought that since it was his first year, he had to get used to going to school.

Then we changed schools, and there was still a problem, so I took him to his doctor. The doctor gave me a paper to fill out and another one to give to the teacher. They filled it out, and I thought they hated my son. Because they added notes, the doctors diagnosed TJ with ADHD.

The doctor put him on medicine. I didn't know what to do. Yes, there are so many books about taking care of a child. But there are no books to tell you what to do when your son doesn't sit down, when the school is calling you because he keeps distracting the entire class. There are no books to tell you what is right for YOUR child.

So, I did what I thought was right for TJ. I was doing what I wanted, and I didn't care what anyone said. I went to the meeting, and

Stacy got mad because she didn't want me to leave the house. She said because I was leaving the kids there. I said I'm leaving the kids with their dad. But then I said fine and took them with me. That was a problem because I still left the house.

Then I just stopped going. One night, I decided to go on a dating site because, technically, I was single. I met a woman named Candy. I told Jay that she was coming over. He said OK, that's fine. Stacy, on the other hand, had a fit and yelled. I guess she thought I was going to get over this lesbian thing and get back with her nephew.

Candy left and called me. She was mad that I had her come there, and my aunt yelled at her. I went to the kids and my room and cried. I knew I wasn't going to be able to be myself there.

We live so far out of town, so we decided to move closer to town. When we did, things got worse. Stacy started about everything. I was again walking on eggshells. This time, I made sure Stacy knew I had people. I had family that was on my side.

The day I moved, my aunt Tosha called me, and she had some money for me. She said she was trying to get in touch with me. I told her that my phone was on107 and to send it to Western Union she did. I went to get ready.

Stacy didn't believe that I had money coming to me. I just got ready, and I left to get it. I got a new phone and stuff for the kids. Stacy was very jealous. But I was not her; I got something for Ella too. Because Ella was my baby, too. I got toys for the kids for Christmas.

Then, one day, I needed diapers for Johnny, and I didn't want to ask Stacy. So, I texted my aunt Lizzy, and she sent it. Again, I went to go and get it. Stacy

said that I was lying no one was sending me money I showed her the text on Facebook and asked Jay who was the people I was talking about. He told the truth and said, my aunt. Stacy got mad because I didn't need her.

I left and got the money and came back with what I needed and a pack of cigarettes. This time, when I tried to give Ella her stuff, Stacy said no, she doesn't need that. I looked at Ella and felt bad. So, I said Stacy, all the other kids have something that's not right. She said no.

Chapter 19 – Being Who I Was Meant to Be

I never got back with Jay. But soon I called Candy again and this time Stacy acted nice. This time, when Candy came to see me, she brought her twin sister Brandie. I went to her car up the block, and she asked if we could go somewhere and talk. I said yeah but I wanted her to know that I had kids, so I said I had to go and get my kids. But when we got there, two out of the three were asleep. So, I took Shanta with us.

Candy brought food for Shanta, the other kids, and me. She said she had to go to work, so we left she took me and Shanta back home. Candy worked at Dominos. Just know I wasn't ready to date anyone. I just wanted to date a girl. I wanted to be myself. But it was too soon. Anyway, she told me she would see me later. I said OK.

I took Shanta, and we went to the house. I put the food for the kids in the refrigerator. I took Shanta, and we went to bed. I didn't say much to anyone. Stacy was trying to be funny, and she asked if I had fun. I said yeah, it was great.

Stacy also said, "It's ok, JJ. She just used you until the kids were old enough where she could take care of them herself." I said that doesn't make sense; I have a 1-year-old.

One day, I had to take TJ to the doctor, so I decided to go and see the lady who took us in. But she didn't answer. I knew she was there, though. So, me and TJ just walked away after saying out loud I loved her, and I was sorry I hurt her. One day friends of Stacy were having a hotel party. It was a pool party. And I liked one of the women. So, I said yes, I wanted to go. Stacy just had to say that Jay and I broke up and that I was going out with this girl named Candy, the one I liked, and her sister both said, 'Aisia, you are cheating on me." The sister I laughed o110 . But when the one I liked, my Bell, came out. If a Bell is reading this, you know what I mean. For everyone else, I mean, I started flirting.

But then I realized that Candy never came so I called her. She told me that she had come, and she overheard everything. I asked what she was talking about. Even though I knew what she meant, she said I heard that girl say you were cheating on her.

She said Aisia, what's going on. I told her that it was a joke and to come. I said I'm with you, right. She said yeah, and she came. She picked up me and the kids. I sent the kids in, and Candy and I talked. I got her to calm down. Then I went inside. But from that moment on, Candy did not trust me. And to tell the truth, she shouldn't have. I am writing this book to tell the truth, and the truth is I wasn't ready to be anyone's girlfriend. But Candy didn't want me either I believe she wanted Stacy.

Anyways, let's go on. Soon, Candy and Stacy started to talk. Candy told Stacy that she feared her at first. Stacy said yeah, she was having a bad day that day.

At this time, Jay wasn't living with us. Then, the same two girls needed to live with us. So, I told Candy what was going on. She thought everyone wanted me. But the two ladies and their mom came to live with us, which was fine with me. The woman I liked was named Anita. Anita and I got close. We would go to the store together we would do a lot of stuff. Candy and I moved farther apart. Any time she wanted to go somewhere, she would always say Stacy, do you want to go. I would think, what about me? I was like hello, I'm your girlfriend. But I wasn't any better.

After Anita, her sister, and her mom moved in, I had to go back to Candy and tell her that my ex-boyfriend, my kids' father, was going to come back to live with us. She must have thought I was playing games with her. Because she then said I can't wait until we move in together. And when we move in together, I want you to put the kids to bed on time. I looked at her like when we said we were going to move in together. It was my first time learning the lesbian U-Haul.

One day, Candy brought her twin sister, Brandie, over. We all hung out and played spades. Things started off good. I was being nice to Brandie because I wanted her to like me. No, not like me that way. But know that I was good for her sister. But Candy didn't like that because they had some issues. To be identical twins, they weren't very close. Because Candy was out, and Brandie was very much in the closet.

You probably want to know how I need that. Well, gay knows gay. So anyway, we were playing spades, and Brandy kept talking, but Candy didn't know how to play, and she would say some other stuff. Candy started to get mad.

So, I took her outside. I talked to her and told her that she was doing too much. She said Brandy was being very mean. I said I know, but she doesn't know us, and you are embarrassing her in front of strangers. She asked who side I was on. I told her hers, but her family is super religious, and she even said her granddad was a pastor. I asked her how your sister would feel about me if I would just start yelling at her. She said that I was right I told her to calm down and let's go back inside. So, we did. I told everyone that Candy calmed down. Starr said that I didn't say anything. She said I probably just said, your right, it's ok. I said whatever, Stacy.

Candy and I started to sleep together. Yes, that's right, I didn't sleep with her right away. The problem was Candy, like Jay, couldn't keep her mouth close. She would tell everyone I was amazing.

Stacy would say how is that possible when Jay would say I was terrible. I said Well, that's because he was a guy. But I didn't like talking about my bedroom life. I'm a very private person. I guess it was because my mom made me that way when I was a little girl. Candy didn't realize what she was doing was getting Anita more interested in me.

Anita would say so, Aisia, you know what you are doing. I laughed it off. I said of course. But I didn't want to talk about it. Candy would tell Stacy and me that one of the First Ladies in her church was the one who taught her how to have sex. I was shocked by that. She would say she was a little girl. Then she said she missed her, and Stacy reminded her of the lady. That's why I said she wanted Stacy, not me. Stacy said that's not that bad. I looked at Stacy.

I thought If she was a he, then it would be bad, right? Then why is it not that bad because she is she? A pedophile is a pedophile. Anita asked me if we could have a three-way. I went to ask Candy. Candy obviously said no. I thought if I said Stacy instead of Anita, you would say yes.

Soon, I started to hate how Candy kept telling all my business. She said she didn't understand why I had a problem because I called Stacy, my aunt. I told her I was a very private person. But she didn't understand that. She was a very open person. And whatever was in her mind, she said it. She was also very mean to me. She liked to boss me around.

So, I decided that I had to do something and soon because she was falling for me hard. So, one night, she was supposed to come over after work. But I didn't want her to come over. I didn't want to be anyone's girlfriend. So, I texted her and broke up with her. That's right, I broke up with her over text. I did it because I was too much of a punk to do it face-to-face. So that was that I was single. But no, I didn't go back to Jay.

After a couple of months, Anita and her family got their own home. But before they did, Anita asked me to be her girlfriend. I said yes. She said she only had one request it was that I didn't tell Stacy. I told her I would. But then I thought Stacy was ok with me being gay. So, I told her I had another girlfriend. She asked who.

I said, Anita. She didn't like that. I told Anita that I told Stacy. She said I was being stupid and that Stacy wanted to be my girlfriend that's why she broke up Candy and me. I told her that wasn't true. She said forget and that we were nothing. I said fine. She and her family left. The day she left, I tried to get her to talk to me. She didn't. They just left. I felt terrible. Then Anita came to the house to pick up something. When she came, I thought maybe she would talk with me. You see, I know how to use my words. I knew how to get people to do what I wanted when I used my words. And Anita knew that, so she didn't say anything to me. Until she left and said bye to Aisia. I said bye. Then I ran outside to see if I could talk to her. But she left.

I then started to fool around with the next-door neighbor. Stacy found out, and she ran with it. Stacy didn't understand this fooling around thing. She was used to having one partner, and that's it. One day, we were having a party for Stacy's birthday.

Stacy wanted to go and get Anita and her family. We went, and Stacy went in before me. She told them that I was fooling around with the neighbor. I walked in in the middle of it.

Stacy walked out with Anita's mom. I turned around to walk outside when Anita grabbed my arm. She said that Stacy said that I was fooling around with the neighbor. And how was she supposed to feel about that? I said wait, you said we were nothing. She said that I knew she didn't mean that. That's when I realized women are confusing. But with her saying that I was motivated to make Anita mine.

Chapter 20 – I Have To Leave

Soon, Stacy and I were arguing a lot more. I hated living with her. She would complain about this or that. I went back into the hospital for a second time. This time, I took an overdose. I got a call from Stacy. She lied and said my baby boy took one of my pills. I went to another hospital, and the counselor told me to leave. She said you're not going to live if you stay there. While I was in the hospital, Stacy called my mom and sister and said I was talking about them and that they should take my babies because all I cared about was women.

While I was in the hospital, the counselors and doctors asked if I had somewhere to go. I told them I could live with the kid's grandma until I leave when I get my money. When I left the hospital, they reminded me to just walk in and get my kids and leave. I never had all the people in the hospital beg me to leave somewhere, not even when I lived with my mom. So that is what I planned to do. I got to the house, and I went in.

Jay said she was home. But I went straight to my room. My baby was lying down asleep. I packed the kids' stuff and then went to pick up my baby. He woke up, and I started to play with him. Jay walked in and saw the bags. He said what are you doing. I told him I had taken the kids and I was leaving. He got so mad he choked me. My baby hit his head. Then I yelled. Stacy came in and caught Jay in the act. He jumped. And Stacy asked him if he choked me. Of course, he said no. I said yes, you did. I check my baby. He was ok. I got up to go and called the cops. Stacy said she would be on Jay's side. I thought, of course, you will. So, we decided Jay would leave.

Remind you that was for the time being. Jay went to live with his mom. Soon after that, Stacy came to me and her boyfriend at that time that Jay was being kicked out and he needed somewhere to live. I thought to myself ok, so you don't care if I feel safe. But I said OK, he could come back because they already made up their mind. Actually, what I thought was that fine, HE'S YOUR Nephew. What I meant was he was her nephew, and I was nothing to her.

I didn't know how much Stacy didn't care about me, but I was soon to find out. Jay moved back in, and I was too scared to stay there all day, so I would drop off my son at school. Then I would go to Anita's house. Not to get with her but to just get out of the house. I would do this every day. Then, I would go and get my son and go back to Anita's house. On the weekend I would spend a night out at Anita's house or the kid's grandma's house. Anywhere but at that house. I didn't feel safe. Stacy didn't like this. I didn't know, but every time I complained about Stacy with Anita, her family would tell Stacy behind my back.

One night, I came back, and Stacy broke my TV. I didn't want to fight that night, so I got up to leave. I hear Stacy say to Jay she's trying to leave. I didn't say anything. I walked out of my room, and jay said give me the food stamps card. He knew the next day was the day I got the food stamps. I told him no, I was going to go for the night because I don't feel save here. He pushed me repeatedly. I told him to stop and tried to hit him so he would stop. He held me up so I could move. Stacy walked past me and laughed. I looked at Stacy, bragging her to get him to stop. But she didn't.

Jay's dad got him to stop pushing me around. I got away and I saw that my oldest son saw everything.

I yelled at Stacy, "You're a woman why didn't you help me."

And she just shrugged her shoulders. I said I was going to go to the cops. And they all said they were going to say I lied. And because I have bipolar, no one would believe me anyway. I walked to Anita's house. They didn't believe me and just told me to calm down and go back home. I thought that's not my home. I stayed for a little while, then went back there. I cried all night long. My baby girl saw this. Anita asked if I could help do something the next day.

So, I got up, took my son to school, and went to do the thing for Anita. The kids and I were outside waiting when a lady came up to me. I didn't know this lady. She just saw the kids and saw that I looked distressed. So, she came up to me and said she wanted to give me something for the kids to have breakfast. I told her thank you, but I have food stamps, so they can eat. I tried to smile while I was saying this.

But then my Baby girl, who was three at this time, said, "Daddy was being mean, and mommy cried last night."

The lady looked at me, and I said I was fine, and again, I tried to smile while saying this. The lady gave me the money anyway, and I thanked her and said God blessed her. I was still early so I told the kids to McDonalds. I got them breakfast. I sat there and looked at my babies. I knew I had to leave, but I had to do it smartly. Soon, it was time to do what I had to do. I did it, and I went back to the house.

I told Stacy that I was leaving on the first. She asked how when I called your mom, and she said you couldn't go there. I told her that I would find a way. She said you know you can't be raising the kids by yourself. You know you're going to get overwhelmed, and it's going to be too much for you. I said we're see. And that was that.

The problem was it was the 17th of the month, and I had weeks to go. But I never changed my mind. Because once I put my mind to something, I'm going to do it. Even when one day I was at Anita and Stacy came there and she started a lot of drama. She even called my ex-girlfriend Candy and got Candy to back her. I called my aunt Tosha and told her I needed my uncle. She told me to come home, but my uncle couldn't get to me. I told her I would come home. She said it again, but this time, she said Iesha, come home. I said I am. I also texted Diana.

I been in contact with her while I was down there. I thought it's only been two years, so she was still my best friend. But she didn't text me back. But I thought nothing of it. I did go to the cops. I asked them if they knew of a d.v. Shelter. Dv stands for Domestic Violence. The cop said he thought there was one in Columbia. But that was another town, and I would still have to wait. Stacy did everything she could to try to break me. She kicked me out of my room. She put my stuff outside. She would say little things. But she didn't break me. She didn't make me change my mind. Jay's dad tried to get me to leave my daughter down there, and he said he would bring her to New Jersey the next month. I told him no, I am taking all my babies. We slept on the floor. But I put pillows under the kids so they can sleep comfortably.

Then, it was finally the day that I would leave for good. I got up to take my money out of my bank. Stacy then tried to give me another dig; she said oh, Shanta broke Ella's tablet, and you owe me. I said OK, with a smile on my face. I went and got the tickets for the kids and myself. I got Stacy's money out, and I got myself a phone. Because Stacy broke the one I had, I went back to the house. I gave Stacy the money I said goodbye to everyone, and I left. We grabbed our bags and walked out. I didn't leave Sumter until that night, but we left the house that morning. We went to Anita's house. She told me not to come back because she wanted the best for me, and she knew that the best for me was not being with Stacy. I said I wasn't. We stayed at Anita's house for a while until it was time to go.

Chapter 21 – A New Life

I called my mom while I was on the bus. I asked if I could stay there for a little while it wouldn't be forever. She said that I could stay there. I called Essie and told her what happened and that I was heading back home. She said I'm so sorry that happened to you. I also text my brother Antony. The last person I called was Diana. She didn't answer. I then texted her that I was heading back and that maybe we could hang out because I needed a friend. She didn't respond. The kids slept most of the way. That gave me time to think of what I do now.

I planned what I had to do. I knew I had to get on the grid because it was just me now. I had to do what I had to do for my three babies. We got to Newark. We took the train to Journal Square. I called my mom to find out where she lived. She told me, and we took the bus. We got off the bus, and my mom was right there waiting for us.

I started to cry. I texted Diana that I got there safely. She didn't respond. I got back four days away from Johnny's birthday. So, he was about to be 3. I said to myself that the first two years of his life were crazy. The first day we got there, my mom's friend took us to Chuck E Cheese. I was glad that the kids had a good time. Then they brought the kids some winter clothes. Because we came from Sumter, and they needed it. We went to take care of business as soon as we could. I kept calling and texting Diana for about 2 or 3 months.

Until one day I had to go to Bayonne to do something for my aunt Tosha when I saw Diana's husband. I was so excited I said hi. He said hi. I asked how Diana was. He said good. I told him that I tried to call, did her number had changed. He said no, it's the same one. I was crushed. He asked if I wanted him to call her. I smiled and said no, that's fine. Just give her my number. You can tell her to call me when she can. He said he would. I said bye, and I walked away hurt. Because I didn't think Diana would ghost me.

I walked to my aunt's house I did what I had to do for her. When I got back to my mom's house, I cried while I was cooking, so no one saw me. I texted Diana one last time. I said I understand. I hope you have a great life. Bye. Another time, I was in Bayonne with my mom said she had to go into the store that Diana worked at, and I saw her through the door. I waved at her. She looked at me and walked away. I thought if I could talk to her, I could find out what happened. What did I do? I needed her. I needed a friend. But she did not want to be my friend. You're all probably wondering why I texted and called for so long. Well, it's because I don't take hints very well.

I understand straightforwardly. That day at the store, I gave up on Diana. I went on with my life. My family kept saying they would see her. They said she would ask when I was going to her church. One day I said to give her my number, but she never called. So, I went on with my life. One day, I told my mom that I wasn't going to live there for long. I stayed with my mom for six months when I finally got welfare to put us in the shelter.

My mom didn't like it because she said she remembered when Her family was in one when she was a kid. I kept telling her it wasn't the same way as before. The kids and I went to one shelter for about two days. Then we went to another one a few blocks away. When I got there, I was done with moving. I met a couple of friends there. I had three babies, and they were very young, so the shelter put us on the third floor. I paid the rent I put into my savings. I paid some food stamps for food. And I did all this I paid this each month. I got TJ and Shanta in school. So, all day long, it was just Johnny and me. I kept in touch with the kid's grandma From Sumter. She eventually came up here with the kid's youngest uncle. Kenneth. But they went to Shanta's sisters' house in New York. When she got to New York, she came to see us in New Jersey.

We did everything by the books. We were allowed to spend three nights out. But we never did. Not one night. Because I felt like if we could spend a night out, we didn't need to live in the shelter, am I right? My routine while I was there was to get TJ and Shanta up. Get Shanta dressed because her bus came first. So, I would feed her first. While we were waiting for her bus, TJ would eat. Shanta would go on her bus. Then, I would run upstairs and get TJ ready. I would get Johnny ready, and we would go and drop off TJ.

Then Johnny and I would go home. I would feed Johnny, and I would drink a cup of coffee. I would eat if I was hungry. I'm not a breakfast person so much. If I had to go do something, Johnny and I would leave after I packed a bag for him. Johnny was still in diapers. But if we didn't have to go anywhere, I would put Johnny in a highchair. And put the TV on. We would stay in the kitchen for a little while then we would go into the room to sleep. I would get up and get Shanta. My mom would get TJ. Then, I would give the kids a snack. While they ate their snack I would cook if it was my turn, or we were they alone. That happened a couple of times.

The kids and I would go apartment hunting. But when I would say

TRA, they would say no. Or they would say no when they saw the babies because the kids were so small. It was like that for a while. I walked hard to find an apartment for the kids and me. While I was at the shelter, I would have to go to therapy, which was fine with me because I just left Sumter, and it was very dramatic. I also took TJ to therapy because he saw what happened.

One day, the kid's grandma called me, and she just said Aisia go to a certain website. So, I went, and I found out that my kids' father was in jail for stalking some lady. I called her back in shock. She said I know, and that Tony told her. I said wow. I asked if his dad knew. Because his dad was still down there, she said she didn't know. That was the happiest day I had at that shelter.

Chapter 22 – My Own Place Again

Soon after that, I got my own place. It was a small two-bedroom apartment, but it was mine. Soon, I got my keys, but I didn't move in until the middle of the month. The boys shared a room, and Shanta and I shared a room.

When I moved in this older lady was outside, I told her hi. She and I got along. My mom helped me to move in. The shelter has this program to help me with free furniture. They gave me beds for all of us, a table and four chairs, two chests and a microwave. The first night there, my mom stayed with us. I was so happy because I did it.

All my hard work paid off. My mom helped me with the babies. An upstairs neighbor gave me a sofa and loveseat, so my house was coming together. Then, I thought I was going to be friends with purple in the building.

So, I thought it was a good idea to tell a lady who lived in the building with her wife that I was gay, too. She said oh, ok. Then I went back to my house. I then heard a knock on my door. It was her wife. She told me that she was ready to fight and that her wife was not interested in me. I tried to tell her that I didn't like her. And I don't like studs. I tried to tell her that I like femes. But she was not trying to hear me. She just kept cutting me off.

So, I just let her talk. Then she told me to stay away from her wife and stop asking her for a cigarette. I said OK. I never talked to her or her wife again. They would call me, but I didn't just say anything to them. They would try to get me kicked out of the house. I befriend a homeless lady. I would let her go to the bathroom in my house. But they didn't like a homeless person in the building, even if it was my house.

Two of the kids were going to school right up the block from us. We lived happily I was finally doing it by myself. I was not following Jay or Stacy around. I was content with my life. My daughter graduated from kindergarten. It was great.

The kids were happy. They got to see both of their grandmas. I was happy, too. We even went back to the church that I grew up in. It was great to take the kids to church. And not only the church but the same one that I went to when I was little.

The next year came, and Johnny started pre-k. He went to school all day, so I was bored. One day, I didn't have any pasta sauce. So, I decided to make it homemade. It made me think of Maegan Morrow. I never stop thinking about Meagan. I would bring her up all the time. So, I looked her up on social media.

Three people came up, but one of them looked like her. So, I texted her and said Hi, my name is Aisia Bell, and I went to the Kare house with a girl named Meagan. Is that you? And I waited. I knew that if I used the spelling like the Kare house used it would really help me find her. I didn't have to wait long because the next day, she responded and expected my friend request.

Talking to her again was just like we never were apart. One day, I was bored so I went to the shelter that got us the apartment. I was talking to one counselor, and she said she was going to do something for me. And she did something for me that would change my life. She got me into a program that helps people get a job. So, I got into the program. The program sent me to another one that helped me with training. But first, the first program had me do some tests. They needed to see what I was good at. By the way, I score so high in perspective. Then, I had to talk to a therapist to see if I was ok to go to work. Everything was good to go.

It took a little while for the second program to start because it was 2020. If you know what I mean. So yeah, it took a little while. The lady that was going to work with me called me to start. While all of that was happening, I decided that I wanted to move. I also moved because the building manager came to my door and threatened to kick me out for letting the homeless person in my house. He also said he was going to call the DYFS on me.

Then he said that I couldn't have my kids running through the halls at all times of the night. I said hold up, that's not my kids. They are in bed by 7. So that was a lie. He took that one back and said oh, that was someone else. I said OK. And I decided to leave. Someone who went to my church helped me get my new place.

So, we moved in the midst of everything. My mom helped us move again. The program started, and I was ready. I went to my first work site.

When I got my new place Essie got her first place. I was so happy for her. She and her fiancé/ the love of her life, were getting a place for their family. They had three babies. They had a girl named Imani. They had a boy named Mannie, and they had another girl when I was still in the shelter. Her name was Jayla. So, I was very proud of them both. I didn't know David was in the hospital. Then, one day, I called Essie to see if she wanted to hang out. She said yeah and she asked if I wanted to bio to her house. I said yeah. We met up, and I said that we should go to Mommy's house so we could get food to make at her house. She said yeah.

So, we went to our mom's house, but she wasn't there yet. So, we waited and told our mom what we were going to do. She dictated to come with us. So, we went to Essie and David's new house. We walked there, which was a pretty good distance. When we got to Essie's house, she learned that David was in a medically induced coma, and the doctor wanted to cut off his legs.

Two days later, he was still in a coma. I stayed with Essie the whole time. I didn't know how to get her through this one. I just tried to be there for her.

Soon after that, the doctors took David off life support. So, overnight, Essie became a single mom. I asked the kid's grandma to watch them so I could be there for Essie full-time. I really didn't want my kids to go to a funeral. Essie and I got our clothes, and we got ready to go to the funeral.

One of my cousins and a family friend came. It was great for Essie to have support. She even was surprised to see people there for her. I went up and spoke for David and how I felt about him. The thing is that I don't like to speak in front of people. I get so nervous that I start to shake. Everything was done, and then Essie and I left. Our cousin brought us home.

As soon as we got to Essie's house, my kids called me. They called crying that they were hungry and they were not having a good time. I asked my cousin if I could borrow a couple of dollars to get to New York. I called them back and told them I was on my way. Their uncle called me and told me that he would bring them to Jersey City. So, I got them, and I was just happy to have them. I didn't think about calling anyone.

Since I didn't have to go to New York, I had some money. I took them to McDonald's and went back to Essie's house. I put them to bed and then just relax with Essie.

The next morning, the kid's grandma called me. She asked if I had the kids, and I said yeah, thank you for taking them for me. She said to me thank you for not telling me that you got there safely. I said that I fed them and put them to bed. She said yeah, everyone has their own problem. I said OK. I hang up.

Then the kid's grandma put on Facebook something about no one is there for her when she needs them. I learned later it was not about me. But at the time, I didn't care. I didn't have time to go back and forth about what I wanted to do or what I had to do for my babies. It was just me.

If they grew up to hate me, it was because of me. Also, if they grew up to love me, it would be me. But I wanted my kids to know that if you're able to, then you work. I eventually went back home.

Soon, Essie called me scared. She said, "Aisia, I'm pregnant." I told her to come to my house. We sat down and we came up with a plan We went back to the store and got a pregnancy test. I told her I was there for her, and she knew that. We went through everything together with that pregnancy. We found out she was having a baby girl, and she named her Eden.

Chapter 23 – He Saw Me

I went to my first work site, and it was Garfield Furniture Center. I got there early because I believed if you were early, you were on time, and if you were on time, you were late. So, I was "on time." I just waited for the lady that was going to work with me. When the boss came, he brought the furniture outside. He told me I could sit down. I did but I was ready to get to work.

The lady texted me she was on her way. She got there, and I got my list of what I had to do. I was ready to do everything to the best of my ability. Everything was simple, but I did my best. I went there two different times. The second time the boss saw me. He knew that I could be a good worker. He told me that if I wanted to work, he would love for me to work for him. I said OK. He asked for my information. I gave it to him. I went home so excited.

I called Essie and told her everything. I also called my mom too. I said he saw me. He knew I could be better than just be home. And be on welfare and SSI.

Don't get me wrong, I just wanted to show my kids that if mommy can do it while being a single mom, then they could do anything. I would tell my kids that I want them to do better than me. I wanted them to be better than me. I would tell them this every day. So, I then went to another store to do training there.

I was supposed to go to three different stores, too, but before I got to the third store. The first one gave me a job. Yes, I started working. But it was a lot. I would work, come home, and be a mom. So, I had to rely on my mom. But then she couldn't help me because she had my niece that my sister Mary had. I got to know my niece, Tina. She was very spoiled. But she wanted my mom to herself. It started on the weekends first.

My mom couldn't watch the kids on the weekend. So, me working on the weekends, I would have to take the kids. Then it went to some weekdays. So yes, my boss hated it. Yes, when I was there, I worked hard. I did what he wanted me to do. But when I couldn't call out. But that means no work, no pay. I wasn't getting SSI anymore. I was only getting food stamps, that's it.

So, at this time, yes, we could eat, but we couldn't live. I couldn't pay my bills. So, I broke down. I couldn't do it anymore. So, I called my sister and my mom, and I went to the hospital. My sister took my kids in. Which was great, but my kids are a handful if you have three of your own. In the hospital, I got something I never had. Meagan came to see me. That was wonderful.

Chapter 24 – What Are the Odds

When I got my first apartment after the shelter, I got into the church even more. When one day I was in Sunday school this lady walked in. I later got to know her name was Monica. I noticed everything, so I noticed that she had a boot on her foot. She broke it, I guess. She said his sister. And I looked at her because I never heard that in New Jersey I heard that in the south. I said hi with a smile on my face.

Another time again we were in Sunday school when she raised her hand and asked a question. I loved her voice. Then she was asked to read a part of the Bible she had a wonderful voice. If you don't understand why, well, like I said, I like words. And when she read the words, she brought it to life. I didn't know it then, but we were going to be close. I love you, sissy. But at that time, something was different about her. I didn't know what it was. But I knew I wanted to be closer to her.

Then, I lost the food stamps. So would ask my pastor If he knew where I could go and get food. He told me I should ask Monica, so I did. I was nervous because I started to like her. Then she gave me her number. I took it, and she told me where I could go. Before I even got close to Monica, my daughter did.

Shanta would go to Sunday school, and then she would want to sit with Monica. I would let her. The Johnny sat with her. Then TJ sat with her. So, my family loved her too. They would hear Ms. Monica at first. Then, they would call her Auntie Monica.

One day, Monica and I were talking on the phone. I was telling her something that happened to me when I was little. I told her some of my story. Yes, that's right, this story. She then said something that made me think maybe I could write this book for someone who thinks that they don't have anyone. Or feel maybe they are all alone. She just said What Are the Odds.

What she meant was our life was so much alike but living so far apart. What were the odds that we found each other in this big world? So that's what I plan on doing was writing this book. Before I had that conversation, I gave up on my dream. I gave up on helping anyone. I gave up on ever doing anything with my words. Now I know that I can do it. I told her I was going to write this book for everyone like us.

One day, I went to the doctor with my mom. The paper had a part on it that asked if I felt depressed. I said yes. So, the doctor came in and told me that they couldn't let me go. I got a lump in my throat. I don't know where it came from, but it wouldn't go away. My mom got them to let me go.

But then they took too long, and the lump got bigger. I was nervous because I had things to do, and I couldn't be in the hospital. I had to go and get my son, and I promised my boss to be there after I got my son. So, when I was able to walk out the door, I was happy, but the lump was still there.

I left my mom and went to get Johnny. I was scared that I would be late, so I thought that's why I had a lump. But I got him on time. We started to walk towards my job. Johnny had to use the restroom.

We stop at the corner of my mom's house. As soon as we stopped, it happened.

A car jumped the curb and hit us. I saw the car long enough, and I was only able to push Johnny out of the way, but he still got hit by the wheel. They say when something dramatic happens to you, see your life. But I didn't. I saw my three babies. I saw their faces smiling. That's all I saw. But then I heard Johnny yell that he was going to kill the driver and passenger. So, I knew I had to get up. I knew I had to show him that I was ok.

So, I got up and called my boss. I told him what happened. I called mommy. She didn't answer me. So, I called Essie to tell her. I told her. She called Antony. Antony then got in contact with my mom. I also texted Meagan.

Johnny and I sat down. There were people who all called the cops. The car ran us into a person's house. They ran into the house and got Johnny some juice. He said thank you, but he was shaken up. I was, too. But I couldn't let him see that. I tried to tell him that I was fine. I had to put up a front. I told him repeatedly that I was fine. But I was hurting. I was down. But then I thought that I had been down before. Yes, maybe not the same way, but I've been down before. We went to the hospital and the doctor gave me so many tests.

My mom came with my oldest son and daughter. The nurses took Johnny to another room so I could get checked out. He wasn't sure that I was fine so he asked when I got back to my room could he see me. The hospital let me go. We left, and my mom took us home. The next day I went to my doctor she told me to stay home for a couple of days. I went to Essie's house. She was sad, and I had to tell her that I was fine. I called a lawyer. She helps me.

Essie and I got so close during this time that I knew when Eden was going to be born. One night, I wasn't feeling good. My back hurt, and my legs were hurting. Just like I had when I was in labor with Shanta. So, I called Essie multiple times. When she didn't answer, I called my mom.

So me and my mom called Essie still no answer. My mom called me and asked Aisia what are you going to do. I thought she was your daughter. Why do I have to do something? But I woke up my daughter. And if you have a child like my daughter, you never want to wake them up. I called the demon. Even my boys know not to wake up the demon. She was mad.

We started walking up the block then Essie called me back. Shanta was even more mad. Because now we had to walk back down the block, go back up those stairs, and walk back those the door. I just got the kids back to sleep when Essie called me and said she was in labor. I thought that she was on her own. I wasn't waking up that demon again because I didn't have a death wish.

While all of this was happening, I couldn't keep up with everything, like cleaning and getting enough breakfast food in the house. I had food for dinner and lunch but not breakfast. Also, my son wouldn't put on deodorant and cologne. So, the school is called DYFS. That is very understandable.

They came in, and they opened my case. I tried to do everything that they wanted me to do. But then they put me in this program that

I hated. They just were doing what they thought was right for my family. The program was to teach me had to clean, how to get the kids to help me clean and to help me with my mental health. Which sounds good, right? But the problem was that the boss was someone who "helped "my mom. Let's call the boss, Mrs. Manny. If it was a program without Mrs. Manny there, I would have been fine.

But I have PTSD, so seeing Mrs. Manny just brought up so much stuff. She was very condescending. She would call me by my mom's name. I would correct her. She would give me stuff for the kids, like computers, and ask if I knew how to set it up.

I would look at her and say yes, of course. She would go on and say oh, that's good. But it wasn't like she believed me because she then would ask again if I set up the computers. I said yes. She loved to call me by my mom's name I think she just thought it was funny.

One Saturday, my mom and sister Essie said they would watch my kids. So, I took them there and went to work. I was at work for about 2 hours. When my daughter called me, she said she wanted to come. Then my mom called me crying, and she said to come because Essie baby's dad jumped in my mom's face.

So, I told my boss I had to go. I left and went to Essie's house. I was mad. No, I was mad. So mad that I saw nothing but red. Then my mom called me and said that I didn't have to come. I told her it was too late. I got closer and my niece Tina called me and asked where I was. Was, she said the guy pushed my sister across the room. I said I was almost there. I was around the corner. She said all the kids were outside. I said OK, and they would see me coming. I got there, and all the kids cheered. My mom came out and said he was inside. Then she said her favorite line, Aisia, what are you going to do? I thought I was going to protect my sister. I went in, and I told him to leave. I said first it was her closet door that he broke.

Then it was her eye that he threw a phone at and gave her a black eye. Then, it was her window. Now, it was this. I told him to get out. He said the wrong thing he said for me to make him. I told him, OK, just wait, and I went outside. Then he came outside and tried to get loud with me. I told him to quit because he didn't scare me. Then he tried something else. He said that he had a bad time at his mom's house.

I asked what that has to do with Essie and everyone here. Then he tried to say that I was right and that I should hit him. Now, I'm not stupid. One or two things could happen. He could think, ok, she hit. We could move on now. Or he could be a punk and call the cops on me.

All I said was we're both pieces, so stop the woe is me. I told him I didn't want to hear the poor junk. I was so tired of his woe is me that I just went inside and asked Essie what she wanted me to do. I was hoping she said for me to hit him. But she said she wanted everything and everyone to stop. So, I said OK, got my kids and left. I left mad, but I left.

A couple of months later, I called Essie. When he was there, he said that I didn't like him. I said no, I don't. I said that I thought he was a loser. So, he started a lot of drama. He told me that Essie and my mom were talking about me. How I was so terrible and that I love to start drama. I got so mad that I said fine, they can live their own lives, and I won't be in it. And I stopped talking to them. That's right, I stopped talking to my own mom. But I was tired of being the black sheep of the family just because I knew what was right and what was wrong. I was tired of everything being blamed on me. And I was tired of crying because my kids and I were not being treated right. I was tired of saying it's not fair like a little girl.

So, I just cut them out of my life. But that wasn't the worst part. I asked the lady who came every week if she could pray for my sister because she was in a DV relationship with her last child's father. The lady said she would.

Then Mrs. Manny came and said something that made me believe she knew everything that happened to me when I was a child. She said your mom was abused by your dad, right? I said he wasn't my dad, and yes. I thought if she knew that then she knew what happened to me. She would always bring up this one lady who was an old DYFS worker. The lady was in DYFS to help families. She was there to take money from families.

Well, that's what she did to mine. I told you that the workers that were in my life back in the day were unprofessional. First, the old caseworker told my mom that she would help her get on a budget. Then she took my mom's cards "so she could help her" but then my mom's case was "close, "but the lady was still in our lives. I knew what was going on, and I would tell the truth about everything, so she didn't like me. I knew that.

I knew that this lady was the reason I got kicked out. I knew that my mom told her what was going on with me, and she told my mom just to kick me out. So, hearing her name really brought back those feelings. And I said it. I told my DYFS worker that I didn't trust this lady. I said I didn't believe her. And if she said the sky was blue, I would say she was a liar. I didn't like or believe her.

One day, she had pushed me too far. It's been a year since they opened my case, and I have been done. She came to the house, and she tried to threaten me to take my kids. But I am not my mom. They would threaten my mom to take us, and she would do everything that they asked, but for me, you're going to have to put your money where your mouth is. I knew I was a good mom. I was washing my dishes when I said do what you had to do.

They both looked at each other. And the boss said you don't care. That's when I lost it.

I yelled, "Of course I cared." "I tried to do everything you asked me to do," "I would get up and get my kids ready," "I go to work," "then I would come home and try to clean," "I would be so tired," but I would try. So yes, I yelled at her.

Then they said they were coming the next day. I stayed home those two days. They came the next day, and I was very smug because I knew she thought it would still be dirty. But it wasn't. And I knew she could see that and smell that because we used a lot of bleach. I say we because my mom helped me.

The lady came in and nit-picked at some things. I knew she would. Then, eventually, they stopped coming to the house, and I would have to go to the office. I hated that, not because I didn't want to walk to the office but because I didn't want to see this lady.

I really didn't like her. I felt that she and the people around her back in the day was the enemy. They never helped me. I got so many problems through their actions. Well, really inaction. They never gave me therapy for what happened to me. And I could believe she was still working with families. Then, the lay that I saw each week said something that I knew was true. She said the lady I didn't like was races against black people. I knew that was true. I wanted to tell Mrs. Manny's boss how I felt about Mrs. Manny. But I didn't.

One day, the lady that came each week went on vacation. So, I would go to the office and see someone else. I noticed she was writing down so I would talk about Mrs. Manny. Not nicely, but how I really felt. I didn't care. Because I didn't understand had she still worked with Families.

So, I didn't care what I said was hurtful or mean. I said what that little girl couldn't. I said what that little girl felt for so long. I let her speak because I didn't want anyone to want any other little girls or boys to feel the same way. I never want anyone to feel like I did. No, I'm not saying that it was their fault; I was saying that they knew I told them what happened. They just didn't care about a little black girl. They made the guy's words true. So that's what I believed. No one cared about me. So, I said what I wanted.

Chapter 25 – What Kind of Big Sister Am I

One day, I just got home from work when my mom called me, and she told me that my sister Mary and brother Patrick were taken. I Couldn't believe that. I didn't know what happened. I asked my mom so many questions. Of course, she didn't have the answers. I wanted to get them I didn't understand why they were taken. I wanted to get them. I wanted to know if they were ok. So, I called all the numbers my mom had.

Then, I decided to go to their day program. So, the next day, I went to Bayonne. I went to their program. I didn't get to see them, but I got to ask if they were ok. Then they let me talk to Mary. The first time she called, she was crying because she thought mommy was mad at her for saying something. Something I was talking about was Mary said the husband of the lady's house she went to touched her. But I told her that no one was mad at her. We all loved her. She kept crying. I finally got her to calm down.

One day, I was walking to work. I got across the street when I heard my family song, Iesha, "By another bad creation." It was Winfield or Win. I turned around, and I saw him, but he didn't look like Win. He had the same face and height, but he usually had a fresh haircut. But when I saw him, he had a dread. I said Hey Win, what sup. I gave him a hug. He asked where he was going. I told him I was going to work. He said he was going to work, too. I said OK. He said we should hang out sometimes I said yeah, we should. I went about my day. We never got to do that.

Two weeks later I just got home from work when Essie called me. She said something I never thought or wanted to hear. She asked me if it was true. That's right, that's all she asked. I said what? She said Win's girlfriend put on Facebook that Win died in his sleep. I said no, not Win. He is so full of life. Like I said, he is always on 100. He couldn't be.

So, I went on Facebook. Then I called his cell. I called his cell three times. I told Essie, yeah, it's true. It hurt so much. I still couldn't believe it because I had just seen him. I thought maybe God wanted me to be able to say goodbye. But then the bells were together. I finally got to see Win's sister, Veda. I was so excited to see her.

Even if it was a terrible situation, out of that tragedy, the family gained something bigger from each other back. We got to know each other again.

When I left the dinner, I guess everyone who stayed decided to have a family reunion. I hope that Win is looking down on me and is proud of me for writing this. I can hear his voice singing my song and tell me I got this. I can hear him cheering me on. Because that's who he was. He would believe you even when you didn't believe in yourself for the Win. I love you, Win.

While the union was going on, things between Monica and me became confusing. So Monica gave me her number. And that my kids loved her already. Monica and I got closer. So close that my mom and sister would go through me to ask Monica. So, I would ask her sometimes, depending on what they asked me to ask her. But we would call each other. Then she told me she liked someone I knew for a long time. I could see them together.

You're probably wondering why I say that; well, that's because I didn't think she wanted me. So, I would push her and tell her that she should tell him. I thought that staying quiet would be better than saying anything to her and not feeling the same way. Then I asked Meagan what I should do. She didn't say anything, so I told Meagan that I asked Monica and Monica would tell me after three dates. But Monica didn't really get it until I wrote her a letter. My words helped her understand. I would always write something when I need someone to really understand something.

Then I had a dream about her. I had a dream that she was my wife. I told her this. But it seemed that we were just going back in forth with are we were working toward something or are we were just friends/sisters. Before you ask, yes, she reminds me of Dannie. Then I got outed "again" to the Pastor. I said again because I was told by my Pastor that my mom said something when I first came out to her.

I knew that my mom wasn't happy with me coming out. But I didn't know she outie me. So, in one meeting I got to hear that I didn't have anyone that I could trust. I still talked to Monica. I still talked to my mom.

Meagan told me I should let it go with my mom because it happened when I was a teen. But then I started to think about my teen years. I started to wonder if it all was fake. Was everyone at church showing me that they cared about me because of who I was, or did they really care? I wrote a letter called "Is This Why." I wrote it so fast. It didn't make sense.

But I knew I wasn't going back. I also wonder if that is why I always felt like my pastor's wife didn't like me. I already told you I can read people, and I know when someone doesn't like me. I always felt like she just put up with me. I didn't know what I did, but now I do. Then I got another meeting the only thing is I didn't get a heads up. This time, they just came and told me that they wanted me to come back. They told me just to think about calling myself a lesbian.

They said no one knew, so I didn't have to be embarrassed about going back to church. Then they left. I went straight to texting Monica. I said a lot of things but what I said at the end was I was done with telling her anything. And I stop talking to her. I got closer to going to the reunion. I was excited.

A lot of things kept popping up. My mom no longer helped me with the kids. I almost had to quit working. I had to do everything by myself. I really mean, no one gives me a break.

While doing this, I would have a good time with my family on Zoom. They would have me smile and laugh so hard. I slowly started to talk to Monica again. My sister Mary got me to talk to her. But I decided that she was 100% my sister or sissy like I called her. There is not maybe it could be more. That's how it had to be. I didn't want any other problems. I only slowly started talking about me dating any girl.

Then, the day of the reunion came around. It was wonderful. I had so much fun. It was the first time I saw my mom for more than a few minutes. You see, my mom decided that she wanted to live with Essie when she got kicked out. I told her she could stay at my house, but she didn't want to. And living with Essie was better for Tina because I have rules for my kids. I have them going to bed at a certain time.

Another one of the rules is not to destroy my kitchen with the food. I wasn't the auntie who let her niece do whatever she wanted. She knows I'm also not the auntie who lets someone play around with your nieces or nephews. But I'm also going to tell you how it's going to be.

So, School was closing for the summer, and I needed my mom to watch the kids. But then she said she couldn't because Tina's mom said she had to have Tina. So, I texted Tina's mom and said that I needed my mom to help me. She said that my kids were the problem and that I needed to give my mom a break. I thought, at least I get my kids at the end of the day. I was like ok, my kids are the problem. But the kid you raised is a very spoiled brat.

You have her think the world revolves around her so much every week she gets kicked out of school. The kid you raised talks to my mom like she is the adult and my mom is the child. Oh yeah, my kids are the problem. But I just said fine. I'll do what I must do.

Tina's mom is my uncle's wife. I know I know what that makes her to me. I just won't ever call her that. That wasn't the only time I had a problem with Tina's mom.

One time, she called my mom out of her name, so I texted her and told her to watch her mouth. Then she blocked me, which was fine with me. I didn't like her anyway. Another time I was watching Tina for my mom when Tina wanted something to eat. That was not the problem.

The problem was that Tina had four different things, so I asked if she really wanted it. I said I was cooking something if she didn't eat it. She said she would then she didn't and wanted something else. I told her I wasn't making something else. She said she was going to call her mom. I said go ahead I'm not scared of her.

Tina called her mom, and her mom and I got into an argument. Got so bad that Tina even felt bad. I made something for Tina to eat and waited for my mom to come back home. When she did, I left and went home.

One day Monica and I got to talk about what happened. I learned that it all was a misunderstanding. Pastor and his wife came the second time without her knowing. She also didn't want to lose me. I told her that I wouldn't take the kids away from her. And I never did. I just didn't talk to her. The thing was, I read people. She didn't have the ability to do that. But she did prove to me that I didn't have to put up my walls with her. I'm also learning about the rest of the bells.

One day, I came home from work when I got a paper from the PSEG, and they turned the lights off. I didn't have any money when I went to the family and asked if anyone could help me. They did. Then, my cousin Christine said I needed to ask for help more. I told her I was trying. She just didn't know every time I asked someone for help, I got it thrown back in my face. So, it will take me a little minute to learn it is ok to ask for help.

Made in the USA
Columbia, SC
23 July 2024

03a27fc8-563e-48c5-b0f3-394ca6a987ffR01